MEN OF CHALE

BY DEREK SPRAKE

HENRY ROBERTS, FARMER

DEDICATED TO
JOAN AND GEORGE AVENELL

By the same author:
PUT OUT THE FLAG
The Story of Isle of Wight Carriers 1860 -1960

MEN OF CHALE by Derek Sprake
Copyright © 2006 Derek Sprake
First Edition April 2006

ISBN-13: 978-0-9552916-0-9
ISBN-10: 0-9552916-0-7

Published by Coco Design Co. Publishing
Long Thatch, Town Lane, Chale Green,
Ventnor, Isle of Wight. PO38 2JS.
Produced by Simone Whitehurst, Coco Design Co.

Printed by The West Island Group, Freshwater, Isle of Wight.

CONTENTS

Lowcliffe House and The Terrace. Towards the Needles c. 1900

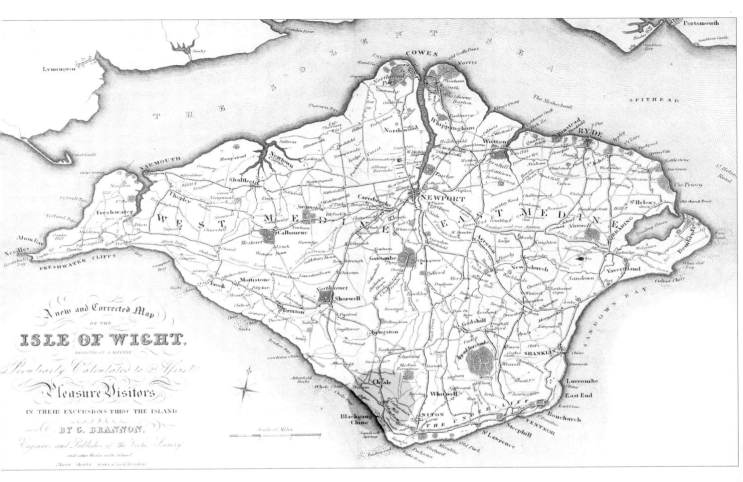

Map by G. Brannon 1847

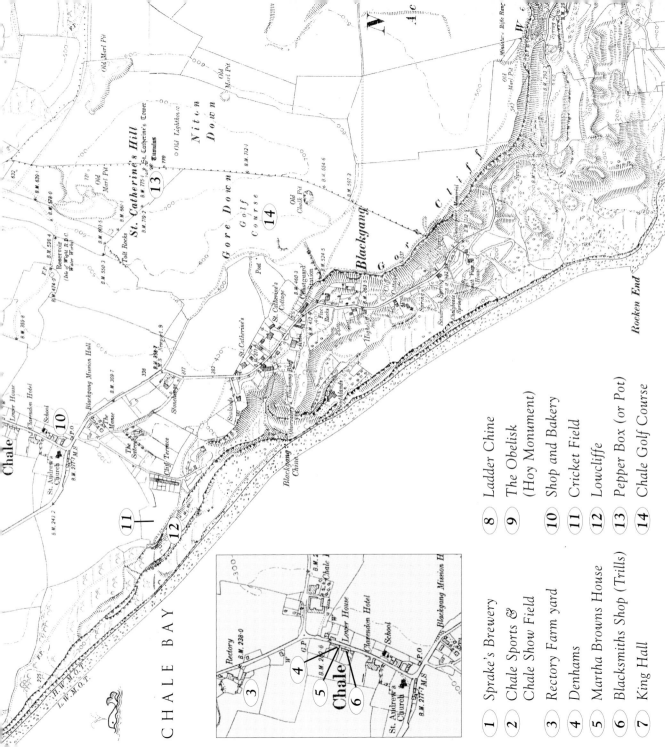

N

CHALE BAY

Watershoot Bay

Rocken End

Reproduced from 1909 Ordnance Survey - Scale 1:10,000

(1) Sprake's Brewery

(2) Chale Sports & Chale Show Field

(3) Rectory Farm yard

(4) Denhams

(5) Martha Browns House

(6) Blacksmiths Shop (Trills)

(7) King Hall

(8) Ladder Chine

(9) The Obelisk (Hoy Monument)

(10) Shop and Bakery

(11) Cricket Field

(12) Lowcliffe

(13) Pepper Box (or Pot)

(14) Chale Golf Course

ACKNOWLEDGEMENTS

The author wishes to thank the following people who helped in the production of this book; by providing photographs and records, and support in many ways, without which it would not have been possible.

First and foremost, to the late Edward Roberts, his parents Henry and Octavia Roberts, and their forbears, who through their inability to throw anything away, have provided me with the records and photographs included.

To Joan, and her husband, George Avenell, who now live in Australia, and to whom this book is dedicated. Joan is a direct descendant of Grace Senior, who married Tom Roberts in 1892, and whose enthusiasm and family knowledge have provided invaluable information and photographs.

To Mabel Nicholson, (Edward Roberts cousin); Roger and Drea Foss; Trevor Chiverton; members of Chale Women's Institute; and other residents of Chale, who provided photographs and the help and encouragement to make it possible.

And to Simone and David Whitehurst in the production of this book.

DS.

PREFACE

"People in Chale always helped each other when they were in trouble". A comment from a long time Chale resident. This was always the Chale way; indeed the Isle of Wight way.

Whether by forethought, or just an inability to throw anything away, when the late Edward Roberts died in 2004, he left a unique record in letters, documents and pictures of a way of life in a quiet Island village which will never be repeated. They provide us with an insight into life over more than 150 years; a period which saw the motor car and the tractor replace the horse as the main means of transport; the telephone and the text message replace the letter as a means of communication; radio and television replace the newspaper as the principle source of news; and two World Wars change life forever.   A period which started with wealthy landowners providing employment, housing and education for the working classes, and supporting the community with philanthropic gestures; and ended with many people owning their own homes and relying on Government to provide for their needs. A time when people did not expect to be paid in money for helping others in need, but who were rewarded by acts of kindness in return.

This book aims to illustrate through those letters and documents how one family, and those who touched their lives, were affected by events of local, national and political consequence, over which they had no control. How they coped with change forced by coastal landslide, and the effects of shipwreck and disaster. And how change in farming methods have decimated the employment of villagers on the land.

Everything here is taken from these records. Gaps in the historical sequence is due purely to lack of information found. The omission of some events, and indeed names, which the reader may know of and will feel should have been included, is purely because they did not appear within the memorabilia. Hopefully this will encourage others to retain and record events from their families lives, for the general interest and benefit of others.

And for those who may be new to our Island, and who are unfamiliar with the locality and its inhabitants, I hope you may gain an idea of how life was once lived, and how it developed over the last 150 years in this corner of the world.

Derek Sprake, April 2006.

Chale School and shop c. 1880

CHAPTER 1

JEWEL IN THE CROWN, AND ISLE OF WIGHT CALVES

Chale, or Cheal as it was formerly called, nestles somewhat precariously on the edge of a fast disappearing coastline near the southernmost tip of the Isle of Wight, and the ill-informed visitor might be excused for dismissing this small village as of little importance. But for those whose families have lived and worked here for generations, it is as special as a Jewel in a Crown.

A sprawling village, Chale stretches northwards from the coast of Chale Bay for about two miles, bounded on the east by St. Catherines Down (and in some parts known as Chale Down), and to the west by a basin of gently sloping agricultural land. Even in the early part of the twenty-first century this backcloth is almost unspoilt by residential development or industrial stain, although strictly speaking agriculture is an industry in itself. The natural development of small farms with small fields enclosed by hedge boundaries mainly still survive, albeit there are now no dairy farms producing milk, where once dozens of small dairies scattered the village.

Perhaps one of the greatest attributes of a 'Chaler', is his confidentiality. To real old Chale people; by old I do not mean 'aged' but from good Chale stock, there is a silence in speaking out of turn or 'saying the wrong thing' about another, even if it is true. "You don't talk about that". And I firmly believe that this stems from Chale's most successful trade. The Smuggling Trade. This book will only touch briefly on this honourable occupation which brought an element of wealth to even the most ordinary citizen, and through which 'everyone' at one time benefited. But there developed a secret language, or rather a coded mode of conversation which even to this day those 'Old Chalers' will occasionally revert without realising it.

"Been in today?" may seem an unintelligible question to a visitor (or even more so, an Overner - a person who was born off the Isle of Wight and who has ventured to set up home here) but to a Chale resident will clearly mean "Have you been into Newport today?". Wherever you are, there is an established terminology unknown to the stranger. You 'go up to Chale (or Blackgang)', 'down to Chale Green', 'over to Niton (or Ventnor)' or 'in to Newport', and conversation will eliminate the need for the place name. Indeed, even the use of 'to' would usually be omitted - 'up Chale', 'down Green', and 'over Niton'. To locals conversing together, the simple 'gwin up?' will not only ask 'are you going up to Chale', but will combine the unspoken request 'and can I come with you?', or 'and can I have a lift?'.

Looking further into the terminology used in the various letters and diaries which form the basis of this book, the code gets deeper. In his letters, Henry Roberts refers often to 'up home' and 'down home', and his neighbours to 'over home'. Although when he married in 1922 and moved into the small farm next to his paternal home, 'Denhams', he continued to refer to The Clarendon Hotel where his father and mother still resided as 'up home'. His wife Octavia (neé Sprake) whose family always lived near the Green, lived 'down home'. Home was not referred to as 'home', but Denhams, as it always had been. And to everyone else, Henry's 'home' was still The Clarendon, and gained the reference - 'over home' because all the other dwellings in that area were on the other side of the road.

This code was extended to the old Sprake's (or Star) Brewery situated at the top of Town Lane, a narrow lane leading from the Green towards Newport (the town), and at the crossroads with Top Road; Newport Road (now somehow referred to as 'Emmet Hill'); and Corve Lane. Wherever one was, one always went 'Up Corner'. That meant 'going up to the Star Inn for a drink of beer', because the brewing family lived there in 'Corner Cottage' which became engulfed within the brewery complex, but which remained the family home. It also ensured that overners were kept respectfully confused!

And just to embellish this coded language of Chale, whenever Henry Roberts was referring to residents in his family's hostelry, they were usually referred to as 'indoors'! (Not 'her in doors', or 'them in doors', but just 'indoors'). 'Mrs Brown' would have been a resident of Chale, but 'Mrs Brown indoors' would be a lady staying as a paying guest in The Clarendon Hotel. "I took two indoors for a ride in the trap this morning". Simple, really!

In recent years a term for Islanders has been invented; that of 'Caulkheads', coming apparently from the term of caulking in the building of boats. I had never heard that used until well into the 1970's; in country areas the term 'Isle of Wight Calves' was more traditionally used. Perhaps this demonstrates the greater divide between the northern areas of the Isle of Wight where boatbuilding was prevalent, and the south and west where agriculture has always predominated. Isle of Wight Calves is a much more friendly title!

Why the Natives are called "ISLE of WIGHT CALVES"

"Wot shall us do Bill?"
"I spose there ain't nothin' else but to cut his head off to <u>SAVE HIS LIFE</u>"

At first it would appear there is little to attract one to this quiet haven of our planet. And yet, probably the most visited and well known Island visitor attraction nestles within the confines of Chale.

Few who have ever heard of, or visited the Isle of Wight, have not heard of or been to Blackgang Chine and enjoyed its modern visitor attractions, museums, displays, and gift shops (known until recent years as 'The Bazaar'). But Blackgang is in Chale! And 'The Chine' has contributed to the prosperity of the village and its inhabitants ever since it was first opened to the public in 1843, and is still in the family ownership of the Dabells who were responsible for its early 'commercialisation'. But to the Roberts family they were always referred to as 'D'abels' or 'De Abels' originating from their Huguenot ancestry and French origins.

How we view Blackgang, is perhaps typical of how one might view Chale itself; beauty is indeed in the eye of the beholder! I hesitate to quote from a book written in 1895 by C.J. Cornish entitled 'The New Forest and The Isle of Wight' for he says Black Gang Chine is as desolate and unattractive as the yellow cliffs above it are bright and beautiful! He goes on - 'But Black Gang Chine, which descends for more than 200 feet from the verge to the sea, is a natural channel for the gradual ooze and subsidence of black clay, iron gray marl, and debris, which the streamlet and land springs are constantly diluting till they are set in motion, and crawl in sluggish streams, like cooling lava, to the sea. Its appearance is more strange than beautiful...'.

And yet in a prospectus to attract funding for The Isle of Wight Sanitorium in 1884, situated at Southlands, Blackgang, Chale, it is described as 'truly a most perfect place!' 'In the Winter it is warm, and in the Summer cool. In December the flowers bloom as though it were May, and geraniums, roses, and myrtles make sweet the air of Springtime when the rest of the world is nipped and pinched by the bitter east wind'. The exaggerations allowed in those days to attract money are referred to later.

But if the fame of one small corner of Chale still abounds, much of its former glory has passed into history.

Chale, and its residents, prospered not only from the hidden income which the 'honourable' trade of smuggling brought to its shores. The arrival of a wrecked ship in the Bay was (and perhaps still is) viewed as providence from God (once, I must add, the lives of the hapless sailors had been saved), bringing work, supplies, and reward to the whole population. Here our Chale 'patois' would have simply referred to there being a 'ship in' which to everyone in the district meant there was a wreck in the Bay (Chale Bay) and there was work and reward for all who were prepared to toil for it - if you were quick before the Coastguard came along! The letters repeated later draw reference to the fruits of the sea from which Chale has always benefited.

Chale Church c. 1790

Schooling has been provided to its inhabitants since the eighteenth century, and thankfully still does in the local Church of England School which was built in 1843. The Parish Church of St. Andrew stands proudly facing the power of the Atlantic winds, and its ancient Churchyard still welcomes those who fall at rest after their lifelong toils.

Sport once abounded to entertain the inhabitants of Chale, with cricket being played on the cliff edge in a field known to this day as 'Cricket Pitch', albeit now 70% a sea of mud descending down the rapidly slipping cliff at the end of The Terrace.

Chale Golf Club provided fine sport on the downs, and although its former Club House still nestles within the trees overlooking Chale Bay, as a delightful private dwelling, its demise was occasioned by both the consequences of major cliff falls forcing a New Road to be built through its greens, and the odd stray German bomb being dropped there as their planes proceeded home after a raid on Southampton or Portsmouth in WW2.

Playing Cricket on 'Cricket Pitch' c. 1890

Chale attracted people from all over the Island to sample good old beer brewed in the village by Sprake's Brewery. Whilst the brewing ended there in 1933, and the Public House - The Star Inn - closed in the 1980's, the buildings remain to this day as residential flats.

The Blacksmith Shop; the Clarendon Hotel (named after the famous wreck in 1836) and other Guest Houses etc.; the Bakery (two) and shops; five or six ale houses; a saw mill; a variety of religious establishments particularly celebrating various forms of Methodism so popular in rural areas; and of course farming and its related trades, abounded within the parish of Chale.

One might well question what is particularly special about all this. Well, perhaps it is the inhabitants, and particularly the Men of Chale, who made it special. Sadly, so much of our heritage and records of every day life are dismissed to the 'skip' or the 'land-fill' these days. But almost by tradition, some have kept a multitude of treasures from their families past - letters, books, diaries, clothes, etc. which reflect the past in a unique and treasured record. One such was the Roberts family of Chale. True Men of Chale. Everything which this book recounts is taken from records and books kept for over 150 years in a small house in Chale, and which reveals the trials and successes of one family and their close relatives and friends.

Whilst many visitors to the little village have included the famous and infamous, including royalty, as we will see, it is surely the unique variety of true Chalers who have placed an indelible stamp on its historic past. Even today, people will say, with pride - 'My family came from Chale'!

One of the oldest occupations is that of the smith, and this is reflected in this name being one of the most used surnames in England. And the most usual smith was the blacksmith. Every community had to have a smith. He made and repaired everything in iron (hence the term 'Black'smith) which was needed both in the home and on the farms; he also made shoes for horses and oxen out of iron; and repaired carts and machinery. The village smith was a very important person.

IW Hunt meet on Chale Green 1907

Exactly when the blacksmith shop near to Chale Church was established is unknown, but around 1835 Charles Brown moved to Chale to take up the business as blacksmith, and it is from here that the dynasty of one of the most influential families to live in and around the area of Chale near to the Church originates. There are many other families who for generations also played as important a role, or even greater, for the good of the old parish at this time, such as Jacobs, Dabell, Cheek, Brown, Wheeler, Spanner, Linington, Russell, and indeed Sprake, (and others). But the Brown/Roberts family certainly played their part as we will see.

When Charles Brown married Maria Morris of Gatcombe in 1832, he is described as 'from Chale' so one must assume that he had been living there, and no doubt was raised in Chale. He became the blacksmith at Gatcombe, and set up home there, where their first children, Frank, and Henry, were born. Perhaps it is a reflection of the educational opportunities available to children who were raised in Chale from around the start of the nineteenth century, that Charles Brown was literate, and had a good style of writing (as evidenced by his account books, albeit that his spelling was more phonetic than 'Oxford'); his wife on the other hand could not read or write (as deeds bearing her mark had to be read to her first).

Having started their family at Gatcombe there was a need to establish a better life for their family. They moved to Chale around 1834 to take over the blacksmith shop there, and to live in the blacksmiths house, the whole being known as 'Trills' (probably named after the previous blacksmith). At first this was rented, but in 1848 Charles Brown bought the freehold, with a Mortgage from the Isle of Wight Benefit Building Society. He died the following year.

Their eldest son and heir, Frank, who was a sailor in the Navy, inherited the property (in those days in the absence of a Will, property passed to the eldest son, and not the widow), but being away from home, his brother Maurice Brown took over the Blacksmiths Shop and lived in the house known as 'Trills' with his mother and other siblings. Maurice became a mason, and bought the plot of land next to their home from his brother in 1854 on which he soon after built the house known to this day as 'Denhams', and into which he moved and lived with his wife.

Charles' wife, Maria Brown, lately widowed, subsequently married a Benjamin Heal, a labourer, and they also lived in part of Denhams.

In the early 1860s, Mary, a sister of Frank and Maurice, married a Thomas Roberts who is believed to have been a gentleman's valet, and they, too, took up residence in Trills, later buying it from her brother Frank. Exactly what happen to her husband remains a mystery, but it is understood he went with his master to America, and was never heard of again. Mary was subsequently described as a widow, so presumably some evidence of his decease must have been established. They had produced one son, Thomas, but Mary Roberts did not re-marry, and became a Laundress, 'taking in washing' in her home to earn a living for herself and her young son.

Whilst Charles Brown had presumably had a good education, which enabled him to read, write, and run a successful business; and his wife was illiterate, they provided (as will be seen) education for his children, and they were all successful in life. Frank, in the Navy; Maurice, as a Mason; Henry who became the Postmaster at Ventnor; Patience, who ran a Boarding House in Chale; and Martha, who became the Infant School Mistress at Chale.

With his sister, Martha, working as the infant teacher in the newly built (1843) Parochial School almost opposite their home, Maurice having completed the building of Denhams, built a 'small' cottage for her between Trills and Denhams, so forming a small terrace. Small was an apt description, as it consisted of just one room downstairs, and one up. This was always simply known as 'Martha Brown's Cottage', and she lived there for the rest of her life. This property was built on land still owned by Frank, and he sold it to his sister in 1882 for £65.

Martha Brown's Cottage, and Denhams c. 1930

Something which was very much part of the way a small country community 'worked' in Victorian times (certainly on the Isle of Wight), and perhaps partly why Martha bought her house, is the care of an orphan. Martha remained a spinster, but clearly loved and devoted her life to children. In 1875, the then Master (head-master) of the school, William Pratt died at the age of just 39 years, his wife having died aged 37 the previous year. Their son, Frank Pratt, was only 3½ years old when his father died, and had started his education at Chale School when just 3, three months earlier, in Martha's class. The school records show that he left the parish shortly after his fathers death, possibly to live with a relative as he was now an orphan. However, the following September, at the start of the new school term, Frank returned to Chale School.

Frank Pratt spent the rest of his life living at or near Denhams and The Clarendon Hotel (then being run by Martha's nephew, Tom Roberts) and working there as a general farm labourer, coachman, and an odd-job man. He also delivered milk and worked on Henry Roberts farm between the two World Wars. However, in her Will (made just four days before her death), Martha Brown, who died in 1904, left her entire estate including her little abode, to Frank. This child-loving spinster teacher who, of course, never had children of her own, had almost certainly 'adopted' little Frank as a child and brought him up under her care. Perhaps a reflection of how casual life was in those days is the fact that whilst Tom Roberts 'bought' (or more correctly 'paid' for) Martha Brown's Cottage, from Frank Pratt, in 1921 for £50, her Will was not proved until 1939, when the property was legally conveyed to him. Life was 'slow' in Chale in those days!

Patience Brown's calling card

Another daughter of Charles and Maria Brown was Patience. Perhaps her name qualified her to run a Guest House, at 3 Cliff Terrace, for many years. Her residence included 4 bedrooms and 2 sitting rooms for her guests. Patience Brown attracted well-to-do middle class Victorian clientele, one of whom wrote in her visitors book "Mrs Houstoun has on two occasions spent several weeks in Miss Brown's apartments and cannot speak too highly of the attention, cleanliness, and comfort which any one occupying No.3 Cliff Terrace is certain to meet willingly". A fine Victorian lady.

The lives of Tom and Grace Roberts, their son Henry, and his wife Octavia, and also the early years of their only surviving son, Edward, are described in fuller detail in the following pages. Their story provides a unique glimpse into how one family influenced the development of just a small part of the little village of Chale. All true 'Men of Chale'.

LAND TAX, INCOME TAX, AND INHABITED HOUSE DUTY, FOR THE YEAR 1874, ending 5th April, 1875.

60

Payable on the 1st January, 1875.

Parish or Place _Chale_ County of _Hants_

No. of Assessment. _114_

RECEIVED of Mr. _R Brown_ the _19_ day of _January_ 1875, the Sum of _One_ Pounds _Two_ Shillings and _Eleven_ Pence for Taxes, as above, the particulars of which are stated in the margin.

William Ratt COLLECTOR.

	£	s.	d.
Land Tax			
Income Tax.— Schedule A, at 2d. in the pound		2	
Schedule B, at 1d. in the pound			
Inhabited House Duty		18	9
£	1	2	11

N.B.—The Income Tax under Schedule A. is in respect of the Annual Value or Rent of the Property. If the whole of such Annual Value be payable to the Landlord as Rent, he is to allow thereout the full duty charged. If part only, he is to allow the duty on such part, and no more. The deduction must be claimed out of the Rent paid next after the date of this Receipt, which must be produced on the claim being made.—Any person refusing to allow the deduction is liable to a penalty of £50.

W. BLAKE, PRINTER, NEWPORT.

PARISH OF CHALE.

Church Rate of Three Half-Pence in the Pound, from Easter, 1871, to Easter, 1872.

Miss. _Brown._

RATED.			£	s.	d.
	17			2	1½

Received,

JAMES BRYANT, Collector.

Parish of _Chale_

HIGHWAY RATE at **6d.** in the Pound, for the Year 1876-7.

Miss _Patience Brown_

Amount of Rate at SIXPENCE in the Pound, payable January, 1877, viz:

	RATED £	£	s.	D.
House	20		10	0
Land				
Tithe				
Total			10	0

Received

Fred Guy Surveyor.

T. Kentfield, Printer, Newport.

No. _73_ **ISLE OF WIGHT UNION.**

Parish of CHALE, the _30_ day of _Aug_ 1875.

Received of Miss _R Brown_ the Sum of _____ Pounds _10_ Shillings, and _____ Pence, in respect of the **POOR RATE** of the above Parish, viz.:

	£	s.	d.
Rate made the 27th day of July, 1875, on £20 Assessment, at **Six Pence** in the Pound		10	
Arrear of former Rate			
Allowance to Owner at _____ per cent.			
Paid		10	

GEORGE R. LOWE, Overseer.

W. BLAKE, MACHINE PRINTER, NEWPORT.

Apportionate Sum,

PARISH OF CHALE.

Received, the _28_ day of _Feby_ 186_ of Miss _Brown_ the Sum of _____ pounds, _____ shillings, and _Seven_ pence, being the amount of One Year's Tithe Rent Charge, due to Messrs. E. C. Boville and Coulson, the first day of October, 186 _1 - 72_

by _Jas Bryant_

Agent for Messrs Boville and Coulson.

£ 0 - 0 - 7
1 - 2

The taxes paid in Chale - 1870's

1841
March
11

2 Lingth in tras — 2
6 Lingth in 3 traces — 6 3
nurt t. Scru t. jor weal — 3
Cruck & lingth heaus — 2

12 2 Shous teem — 4 0

13 4 Shous teem — 2 0
menden Caster t. Chean — 3

15 3 Lingth in 2 traces — 3
putting in prong — 2

16 new weat how — 1 6
Old Shou teem — 4
Cruck & lingth plow Chan — 9
putting in 2 heams cruck & lingth
& peecing 2 Steapls & Key — 1 8

17 Cruck & 3 lingth in tras — 9
menden Cluters — 6
4 lingth in 3 traces — 4
menden 4 Candel Stiks
& Scospan Cover t. hotel — 1 8

18 menden Casting Iron st. hotel — 1 6
peecing t. Taken Cters — 1 0
nosing t. Shears — 1
2 Removes hat — 4
menden Lock feas — 3
Lingth plow Chan — 4
4 Lingth in 3 traces — 4
menden Cluters — 6

19 4 Shous hakney — 2 0
haysing weat how — 6
2 meanger Steapls — 6
4 Shous teem — 2 0
menden Bit t. Brodel — 6

20 3 Shous teem — 4

CHAPTER 2

CHARLES BROWN, VILLAGE BLACKSMITH

The arrival of Charles Brown, his wife Maria, and their children Frank and Maurice, in Chale in 1834 to take over the Blacksmith's Shop, at 'Trills', marked the arrival of a family who would influence the village for a century and a half.

It is their forethought to never throw anything away, a trait which passed down to their successors, which has enabled me to compile much of this book from actual records, letters, and in Charles Brown's case, invoices and notes written in his own fair hand. As will be seen, whilst he kept everything, he also 'hung on to' his money as long as he could, by delaying payment of his bills as long as he could! What changes!

The business was most certainly successful if his account books are anything to go by. His previous education had taught him the basics of life, and whilst now out of living memory, his spelling no doubt reflected his mode of conversation, including the use of Isle of Wight dialect, in his every day life. His entries of such as 'menden pek ax', and 'menden the hamel to the scolry dore' (just for the benefit of non-locals, 'mending a peck axe', and 'mending the handle to the scullery door') when read aloud, and incorporating a slowness of speech, and a 'local Isle of Wight accent' now sadly almost gone except for some of the older generation who survive from when such pronunciation was normal, will demonstrate how he must have sounded. "Tha'tel beee zix pense ver menden yer pek ax, you". "Yur tis, Chaaar, thank ee".

Charles and Maria clearly wanted to provide their children with a good education, and an invoice dated 1845/6 from a W. Deacon to Mr Brown for 'Educating Master Brown' shows that they were both able and wishing to pay for private education. It includes:-

Table book	1d.
Slate, pencil and holder	1½d.
India rubber and slate pencil	2½d.
2 table books (1 for home)	2d.
Firing per Quarter Day (Xmas, Lady Day, etc.)	10/6d
(I can only assume 'firing' was 'school fees' per quarter) And homework too, 1845!	

The dates of the account books range from approximately 1839 to 1847, and include separate accounts for local farmers, although most of his work seems to have been for Mr W. H. Jacobs, farmer of Chale Farm, whose farmland surrounded the Blacksmith's Shop. I have selected just a few entries by way of examples to indicate the type of work undertaken, and the prices charged at that time. The 'translations' shown are simply to help the reader understand some of the work Charles Brown did.

The following are all for Chale Farm.

Cuting a scru (screw) to a Plow (plough) .... 3d.
Fitting a spread to a stone cart...1/-
(a spreader was a piece of wood or bar between the chain traces of the horses in a team of horses)
Putting in a Botcan (?), 4 shets, and one length of caping..1/-
Nozing 2 shars (repairs to front of ploughshare) ....1/6d.
New nut to bolt to a plow 2/-
Laying a Colter One Iron ....9d.
(A colter was a cutting knife fixed to the front of a plough beam to cut the grass ahead
of the ploughshare)
Making a prong...1/3d.
(you did not go into a shop for a new prong, the blacksmith made one for you!)
Sharping (sharpening) a prong ....6d.
Menden clutters..6d.
(Clutters were part of the tackling of a plough or harrow, drawn by a horse).
2 shoes & 1 remove - poney (pony)...1/2d.
2 lingth in a tras..2d.
(two links in a trace - two rings in a chain forming the trace of a piece of harness)
Menden britchen iron ....3d.
New band to a Ceart Weal (Cart wheel) ....£1.4.3d.
(now that's a lot of money!)
4 shoes for a team (a team of horses - two or more horses to pull a cart or plough)..............2/-
Puting in heam strap (part of harness) ....10d.
Peecing spindel ....6d.
2 shoes hak (hack - a general purpose horse) 1/-
2 lingth halter chane ....2d.
17 pins to ceart ....4/6d.

1 lingth in halte ....1d.
Menden dust screen (*in thresher*) ....1/6d.
Making chimbley (*chimney*) ....7/6d.
Chimbley door 2/-
Menden reak to Brick reel (*rake for brick kiln*) 1/-

The following items were for a Mr Brooks, and others. They are items for more general use, probably for a carpenter.

Menden stov (*kitchen stove*) 3/-
Sharping chisels and ston ax (*sharpening chisels and a stone axe*) ....6d.
Menden iron fencing 4/-
Menden fier pan (*mending fire pan*) ....6d.
Menden lock and key...1/-
Oltring iron to geat (*repairs to a gate*) ....1/6d.
Menden pek ax (*peck axe*) ....6d.
Menden water pot (*a kettle?*) ....3d.
Lots of - shoues (*horse shoes*) @ 1/- for two or four; also 3 shoues donkey
(*did he only have three legs!*)..1/-
also - shoues hors (*shoes for a horse*)
Menden scoopen cover 1/-
Menden shaves to fourweal (*shafts for a four-wheeled wagon*) 1/-
14 hucks and 7 curten rods (*hooks, and curtain rods*)....................3/-
Bar to grat (*fire grate*) ....1/6d.
Iron for new reak (*rake*) Must be for a farm hay rake...........................£1.5/-
Making Spugel (*Spudgel - a small bucket with a long handel used for bailing out water*) ....9d.
Menden the hamel to the scolry dore (*see above!*) ....6d.
2 staples & hasp to a foals cup (*fowls coop*) ....8d.

In addition to his account books recording work done, Charles Brown kept many invoices for goods he bought. It is interesting to note that many of the invoices start with a balance forward; or "Left to pay", indicating that he was usually slow to pay, and only paid what he could off his bills! The acknowledgement of payment was usually endorsed with the term "Settled" rather than "paid", followed by a signature.

Here are just a selection:-

Iron Goods - From T.M.Hobbs, Iron & Tin Plate Merchant & Wholesale Ironmonger, 46 Quay, Bristol - 'No packages returned'.
Dated 7th August 1844

50 bars of	?		£7.18.2d.
1 Bale	do		4/8d.
(other goods, descriptions unreadable)			
2 Bars of Coach ap 5 Steel @ 24½oz			7/-
1 Bale	do 26½		£1. 0.7d.
	Insurance		4/-
	?		2/6d.
			£9.16.11d.

Sir, The above completes your order. Your further orders will oblige.

Sir,   Yours obediently.
Abraham Baker for T.M. Hobbs

From Bull & Son, Wharfingers

38 Bevs iron	
1 bundle square rods	
2 bundles hoops	
1 bundle steel	
1 bundle Shur (?)	18/1d.

From G.H. Pettigrew (late Gardner, Nicholl & Petigrew of 38 King Street, Snow Hill) of 23 Skinner Street, Snow Hill, London. Ironmongery of all kinds, wholesale, retail & for Exportation. Coffin furniture from the lowest to the most expensive description. Tools in great variety. (This bill is dated 18th February 1850, and addressed to Mrs Maria Brown, Charles Brown's widow who was by now running the business).

2 bars of Eng	1.3.13	8/-	15/1d.
1 bar of metal	3.22	9/6d.	9/-
2 bars do ½ of	2.10	11/6d.	6/10d.
Carting			6d.

Per Ford & Co.

From Jerermiah Lowe *(his spelling!)* later, of The Clarendon   1845 -

1 gallon bread	anything between 7d. & 1/4d.
2 our tea	7½d.
1lb our bacon	8d.
½lb sugar	4½d.
2 our Coffe	3d.
Blacking *(for the kitchen stove)*	6d.
½lb candles	3d.

The reference to 'our' before tea, bacon, etc. was presumably their own brands, rather than proprietary brands. Most of these items seem to have been bought at least twice a week. Other items in the family diet - vegetables, cakes, potatoes, etc. would have been made or grown by themselves.

From John Newnham

2 quarts Milk	3d.
1lb butter	costing 1/- to 1/4d according to season
1 weeks wash	6d.

From James & John Ticker, Coal Merchants, Coppins Bridge Wharf, Newport - Wholesale and Retail Dealers in Hops. *(the hops were for the numerous local breweries at the time)*

every week - 2 or 3 cwt Coals	1/5d per cwt.

(In 1839, every delivery was by either 'Jabobs Waggon' or 'Rayners Waggon' - local Chale Carriers).

From Edward Way (a local farmer) presumably for animal feed

1 bushel C. Midlings	2/8d.
1 bushel Sharps	3/6d.
1 bushel Barley meal	4/8d.
4 bushel barley *(presumably feed for chicken in view of price)*	1/4d.
1 bushel C. Polld *(probably Pollards, a coarse bran)*	1/8d.

From H. Barton

1 sack of wheat	£1.0.0d.
3 bushels wheat	10/-
1 sack Barley	15/6d.
Faggots (bundle of sticks to light fire)	3/-

One such invoice came to a total of £14.4.3d. Charles Brown owed Mr Barton a bill totalling £17.15.11d. These were settled with a payment of £3.11.8d. Simple Barter which was a common method of trade at that time.

From Dav. Reynolds

1 bushel barley meal	4/-
½ bushel Pollards	1/-
grinding & 2 bushel wheat	1/-
½ Jack of flour	varied between 13/- to 14/9d.
5 gallons flour	7/-
1 bushel pollards	2/-

From Henry Ralph (A cobbler?)

Boot *(presumably a repair)*	6d.
Leather	1/6d.
New boots	7/-
New boots	5/6d.

And then there was the builder!

From Benj. Jolliffe

2 quarters White Lime	9/-
½ days work	1/4½d.
6 days work - bricklayer	£1.0.6d.
8 days work - labourer	16/-
Taking off tiles, cleaning, pinning, pulling down, and clearing away -	
14½ days work - bricklayer	£2.9.10½d.
6½ days work - labourer	12/6d.
4 quarters lime	18/-
Rebuilding -	
800 single laths & nails	£1.4/-
127 feet of rough paving	£1.14.7d.
125 Fareham bricks	5/4d.

(This work was started in June 1843, and finished in July 1843. Payment was settled by instalments, and was finally paid off in   April 1845!)

From William Jolliffe, 1843.

2 new lead lights		2ft6½ x 1ft2½	12/-
2	do	2ft2 x 1ft ½	8/8d.
Bradding in	do		6d.

(fixing with brads - small nails)

To taking out light and fitting it to Casement, and making light for Back House .... 4/6d.

(making window for outside toilet)

From James Cheverton, 2nd June 1837.

	500 Countefs (Countess) slates @ 13/- per '000	£3.5.0d.
	1 M of 4 H Slating nails	2/6d.
	½ M of 5 H do do	1/6d.
Jan 1847	100 Duchess slates	£1.0.0d.

From Robt. Pinnock, (Linen and Woolen Draper - Silk Mercer & Hosier - Haberdasher, etc. - Family Mourning - Family Linen)   137 High Street, Newport, I.W., 1844.

7½ blue shirting @ 1/-		7/6d.
6½ blue shirting @ 10d.		5/5d.
2 Calico 4½d.	4 print	2/9d.
2½ print	4½ Cotton	1/1½d.
Needles		3½d.
2½ Check	3 Ribbons	2/9½d.
Stays (corsets)		4/6d.
Blankets		14/6d.

And a letter, or rather just a note - dated 29th July 1842

To Messrs Charles Brown,

My Bristol trader is come to call on me today which he would be glad if you will come to Newport tomorrow by one o'clock for he is going away soon after two. Meet at Grapes Inn.

J. Morris

A good home cure

For those who lived in remote parts, with the nearest Doctor a long horse ride away, the home cure was essential, and by all accounts, what was good for you would be just as good for your horse! (or was it the other way round?). However, here are just a few good old fashioned Isle of Wight remedies, or rather 'receipts' (recipes) found jotted down on odd scraps of paper:-

A RECEIPT FOR RHEUMATISM
Take 3 pennyworth of Hartshorn; 3 pennyworth of Apadildoc
(*but it does not say what you do with it*).
However, elsewhere there is another cure for rheumatism.
1 oz Spirits of Ammonia; and 2oz Olive Oil.
Mix them well together until quite white, and rub it in
the parts affected.

FOR GRAVEL (*a complaint of the kidneys*)
Take blackberries when in their red state and steep
them in gin. Take a wine glass full three times a day.

FOR SCURVY
Take a quarter pint of best tar, and a quarter pint of your own
water. Mix together and wash with flannel the parts affected!

FOR THE PILES
Take a sheeps tail and roast it, and let it drop into some of
the Best Tar. (*it does not say what you then do with it!*)

FOR DISORDERS OF THE KIDNEYS IN HORSES
1 oz Sucatilius Balsam: 1½ drachms of Spermacita;
½oz Salt Prunella, and mix together.
If the urine is bloody, add ½ oz Japan earth.

FOR BRUISES
2oz soft soap; 1oz Oil of Bay; 1½oz of Waster of pure
ammonium; ½ oz Oil of Orignum; 2oz Camphorated
Spirits wine. Mix it.

Home cures! - 1960's

28

FOR A BOWEL COMPLAINT, ALSO FOR RELAXATION
2 drachms of prepared Chalk; 2 drachms of Gum Arabac; 40 drops of Laudanum (opium); 40 drops of Sal Valatile; 6oz water. Mix, and take two table spoonfuls for a dose every three hours.

FOR INDIGESTION, WIND, ETC. ETC.
4 drachms Columba; 4 drachms Carbonate of Soda; ½ dracm Ginger; 4 samples of Rhubarb. Mix. Take a teaspoonful in a wine glass of water half an hour before dinner.

FOR A COUGH
2 parts Toola; 1 parts Linseed Oil. Mix and give a teaspoonful, sweetened with sugar, when the cough is troublesome, and 2oz Garlick; 1oz white sugar candy; 1oz Olive Oil. To be beaten together.

FOR THE BILE
2 sumples of Blue pill; and 1 drachm Extract of Colocynth (?) Compound. Mix into 24 pills; take one or two at bed time - try one pill first!!

FOR A FRESH CUT OR ANY OPEN WOUND IN A HORSE, OR MAN.
4 oz Linseed Oil; quarter oz Spirits of Turpentine; quarter oz of Tar. Mix - This is excellent for broken knees.

FOR THE GRIPES (PAIN IN THE BOWELS) IN A HORSE
1 quart warm water; ½ pint soot; ½ pint salt; quarter lb lard Mix - This will very soon cure.

FOR A STRAIN IN A HORSE OR COW
½ oz Oil of Origanum; 2oz Spirits of Turpentine; 1½ oz Liquid of Ammonia; ½ pint Strong Vinegar. Mix, and rub some well in twice a day.

(The author feels he should put a health warning here! If any reader tries any of these cures, and they fail; don't blame me! If they work; patent it).

A Chale School Concert c. 1890 (Martha Brown on left; John Cook (Master) in centre)

CHAPTER 3

Extracts from

CHALE PAROCHIAL SCHOOL LOG BOOK

from 1869 to 1873 and other school records

Whilst Chale Schools (there were two - the Infants School and the Main School) were opened in 1843, the first Log Book starts in 1869! And perhaps the first lines go some way to explaining where the earlier records were kept - they weren't!

The book discovered in the former dwelling which was always known as Martha Brown's House', built between 'Denhams' and 'Trills' (the old residence of the Blacksmith), was kept by the said Martha Brown, the Infants School Teacher. The first entry, dated 1st April 1869 starts thus -

> *Commencement of the School year. No entry has been made in the Log Book before in consequence of the decision of the Committee of council as to the placing of this School under Gov Inspection not being made known before this date.* (So, we must accept that as good an excuse as we can have!)

The first records go on (apparently covering the period up to 2nd June 1869, presumably as an attempt to make some record of what had happened!)

> *- The Master (the Head Master) opened school with an average attendance of 54 including infants. Since then several children have been admitted from the Hamlet of Atherfield and the daily average now arrives from 60 to 80.*
>
> *At the opening of the school the attainments of the children were very low in all subjects and more especially in spelling and Arithmetic.*
>
> *Since the 18th of April about 16 children have been drafted from the infant department; class inspection has been made and the children are gradually improving in discipline and attainments.*

Spelling was not Martha's greatest attribute!

> *The teaching power consists of the Master and an adult teacher for the infants.*

1869 on 3rd June it is recorded that - *Children from the 1st and 2nd classes are taken out to teach the 3rd and 4th clafses in their turns.* (The use of an 'f' for the first 's' was still used at this time). Pupils were obviously being used as teachers. It was also noted that - *The girls have no sewing this afternoon because of the Dorcas meeting take place tomorrow.* ('Dorcas' was a ladies charitable organisation for supplying clothes to the poor) - no point in doing sewing if some clothes were coming the next day!

June 4th - *Dorcas meeting this afternoon on behalf of the Ragged Schools in London. About 20 boys and girls are present, with Ladies from the Neighbourhood. Rather damp weather affects our attendance today.*

However, on

June 7th - *Better attendance today 89 and 85* (morning and afternoon) *Ordinary routine of School work. And the following day*

June 8th - *A tea party at the Dissenting Chapel has thinned the number. 73 in morning and 52 in evening. Dismissed the children half an hour earlier this afternoon as there are only a small number.* I expect she wanted to go to the Tea Party!

On 10th June is noted - *The second clafs appears to be improving in the Arithmetic. The infants also appear to be doing well, and their teacher keeps them in excellent order.* (Nothing wrong with a bit of self praise; Martha was their teacher!)

14th & 15th June bad weather affected attendance with *many absent again in consequence of the bad weather, but a great many might have been at school in the afternoon.* (Where was Martha; didn't she know how many were there in the afternoon!)

17th June - *Very wet again this morning. Many of the children who live farthest away from the school are here today while those who reside near are absent.* (Presumably it was not so wet when those living farthest away left home to walk to school!)

19th June - *Obliged to punish 3 children for mis behabiour in Church on Sunday. also, Mrs Theobald* (the Rector's wife) *found fault before the children this afternoon bout the needlework.*

22nd June - *Rev. C. Theobald visited the School this morning. A few absent due to the hay making. I taught Long Division of Money to the 1st Clafs.*

24th June - *Children attended Divine service this morning from 10.30 to 11.30. Walter Chiverton absent without excuse this morning. He was sent to School.* (Poor old Walter, he didn't like the idea of a bit of Divine service!)

25th June - *20 children absent in consequence of a false report about a holiday ! and on 28th June Coronation Day holiday !*

29th & 30th June - *Haymaking has thinned the School. Children attend Divine Service from 10.30 to 11.30.*

1st July - *Half Holiday this afternoon in consequence of a Teachers conference held at Calbourn which the Master and infant teacher attended.* (Nothing changes in 150 years!)

2nd July - *another Dorcas Meeting this afternoon. Not so many children present at the meeting this afternoon.* (Not popular these Dorcas meetings!)

Over the next week or so, reference to poor attendance due to hay making. *Took the second clafs in Arithmetic this morning. They do not seem to improve very fast.* but

9th July - Heard the second clafs read this morning. They seem to be improving. Average this week 78.

13th July - Only 34 children in school because the weather was rather dull. On the least appearance of rain the greater part of the children absent themselves, particularly those who live nearest the School whilst those who live farthest from School attend.

21st July - Admission of Mary Coleman. On enquiring of Janet Squibb why she came late this afternoon she said her mother would not allow her to come before because she was kept in. Told her she would be dismifsed if her mother did such a thing again. (Does this mean that if she does not come to school she will not be allowed to go to school!)

22nd July - One or two having been punished for staying away without leave and others for coming late I think has done good. Indeed, Martha Brown seems to be getting the hang of teaching, and

On *26th July - Punished Frank Coombs for absenting himself without leave,* but, the next day

27th July - Richard Brown was punished on the hand this morning for neglecting to learn his verses. He was kept back after the others to learn his verses but as soon as the Master left the room he ran out of School. Charles Orchard was punished for refusing to do as he was bid.

28th July - The inclemency of the weather has prevented the children from attending School today. Only 11, so no work according to the time table was done.

The Rector is noted as attending the School regularly.

30th July - Charles Orchard appears at School this morning but in consequence of the uncivil language of his mother towards the Master the boy was sent home till his mother should have seen the Rector.

2nd August - Punished George and Fanny Bull for staying away from School without leave from the Master. I find the attendance both as regards regularity and punctuality is better since the rule has been adopted. but

On *5th August - Obliged to punish Leonard Chiverton and Fred Buckell for telling an untruth.*

There are several references to children being absent due to harvest.

On *11th August - The first and second clafses seem to learn their home lefsons more perfectly of late.*

(Homework at Chale School as early as 1869!) And then

13th August - Broke up for the Harvest Holidays today for 5 weeks.

So Martha has completed her first term recording the school events in the Log Book. If nothing else, she has learned that a little punishment does wonders, even if the parents don't help! The 'Summer' holidays, called then 'Harvest' holidays were later than nowadays, but were clearly geared more to the children working (and no doubt bringing home a few pennies) than enjoying themselves! And I wonder what young Martha got up to during the break - she was aged 30 years at this time.

The schools reopened after the holidays on 27th September 1869 but due to the gleaning (picking up grain after the reapers) still remaining unfinished, many children were absent.

5th October - *Master absent from School to attend Court in Newport, and the School was conducted by Mr Rawlings who reports the children to have behave well during the Masters absence.*

8th October - *Took 1st and 2nd clafses acrofs to Church to practice with the organ from 3.15 till 4.00 p.m.*

13th October - *William Morris being absent this morning was inquired for and this afternoon he appears at School after playing the truant for a day and half. As his Aunt punishes him, the Master merely kept him in after school hours and cautioned him not to repeat the offence. The weather continues to be poor, affecting attendance most days.*

20th October - *Daniel King (13 years of age) is reported to have been kept at home today because it was too cold. Several away on this account. It is to be hoped we shall have a mild winter as the prospect of a good average is very slight.*

25th October - *Admitted Leah Coleman on condition that she was to attend regularly.*

26th October - *Punished Walter Woodford for going home yesterday afternoon without leave* (he was later to become a brave crew member of the 'Catherine Swift' the Atherfield Lifeboat), *also Charles Fowler for staying away he said, because he was kept in and was afraid he should not be back in time.*

27th October - *George Cheek and William King are making some improvement in reading. but the clafs as a whole do not read as well as they ought. I find the want of a Pupil teacher or good Monitor.*

Snow fell on 28th, affecting attendance - *as it was rather cold.*

2nd November - *Explained the structure and contents of the Tabernacle made by Moses to the first and second clafses.*

9th November - *Punished Walter Brown* (later to run the village shop and bakery near the school) *for absenting himself yesterday without leave.*

12th November - *The 3 Lowes from Rocken End are absent this afternoon because the weather is rather dull.*

25th November - *Rose Hendy's mother came to tell the Master <u>how</u> to punish her girl. The Master told her he could not alter his mode of punishment and Mrs Hendy therefore took her girl to the Rector.*

29th November - *Obliged to punish several children for bad behaviour in Church on Sunday.*

2nd December - *Walter Chiverton and Henry Jenkins seems very carelefs over their sums and Mary Thorn with her spelling in dictation.*

6th December - *Punished several children again for misbehaving in Church. Having been treated with very threatening language on Friday evening by the parents of Clara Chiverton who had received some slight chastisement for staying away without leave the Master sent the said Clara Chiverton and her sister home again on their appearance at school this afternoon with a message to their mother that they would not be admitted again till she had seen the Rector or School Managers.*

9th December - *Received a report from Mr Jacobs that some of the boys have been pulling his bricks about. Cautioned them not to go near the yard again. Some of clafs are extremely dull in Scripture.*

Wet and cold weather kept many children away from school.

22nd December - *Punished Fred Draper and Leah Coleman for staying away without leave.*

24th December Christmas Eve and still at School - *This afternoon in accordance with the request of some benevolent gentleman, loaves of bread were distributed among the children in the Upper School, most famileys getting two Gallons. Today we break up for a fortnights Holiday.* (In those days the celebration of Christmas did not start until Christmas Eve, and continued for the following twelve days - the Twelve Days of Christmas).

Having returned from the Christmas holidays on 10th January 1870, attendance was reported as improving. On 13th January Mrs Raulins was stated to have sprained her ankle so could not attend to the sewing (did they really sew with their feet in those days?!)

18th January - *George Grimstone is reported as about to leave Atherfield for Ireland, and the Carr's from Atherfield have not returned to school.*

24th January - *Clara Chiverton came to ask the Master to readmit her to School again. Readmitted both her and her sister on condition the rules of school are to be observed.*

25th January - *Mrs Barton has kindly promised to give Choir Children a tea on Thursday evening.*

28th January - *Elizabeth Hollier to my surpise showed a little obstinacy this morning which soon vanished at the approach of punishment.*

The cold and wet weather continued to restrict attendance, and indeed, Martha stated on 15th February 1870 - *The cold weather seems to have frightened away the children.*

28th February - *Elizabeth Hollier who was slightly punished this morning went home this dinner hour though she had her dinner with her. She has not returned,*

9th March - *Daniel King is reported to have gone to work, but whether for good or not I am unable to ascertain.*

31st March - *The School Year ends today, the average attendance for the week being 77, and for the whole year 69.*

The following day (1st April) is recorded as the *Commencement of the School Year,* with an attendance of 80 pupils, and within a few days, had increased to 86.

5th April - *Alice Wheeler withdrawn from school as she is going back to Ventnor.*

6th April - *The girls with the exception of Kate Sprake have finished each a piece of sewing for Her Majesty's Inspector. Kate Sprake has neglected to finish her sewing at home last evening. She was punished.* (Kate Sprake later married Samuel Green, and they set up home and ran a Lodging House in Ventnor. In 1887 they decided to seek a better life by emigrating to Australia, and left with their four children aged one, two, three and four, and Kate's sister Rosina, aboard the ship 'The Kapunda' which sank following a collision with another vessel somewhere off Brazil. The end of a sad life.)

21st April - *Mr Parsons from Brixton* (Brighstone) *and friend visited the Schools this afternoon and paid us a compliment as to the discipline and spelling.*

7th June - *Some few children absent to see Mackerel caught.*

On 15th June it is recorded that - *It is a very common thing for children to stay away from school in consequence of bad shoes.*

16th June - *William Stewart White was sent to school but returns before he reaches*

27th June - *Harriet Godden is absent on an average 3 days each week and her Mother complained that she learns no needlework. How can she learn if she is not present.*

28th June - *Coronation Day holiday.*

Into July 1870, and haymaking is again affecting attendance, and the weather is still wet and foggy.

8th July - *Some of the first clafs seem to have forgotten their Chatechism again.*

11th July - *low attendance. There is a Tea Party at the Wesleyan Chaple and a great many children are gone to it.*

12th July - *Punished B. Brown and C. Fowler for absenting themselves without leave yesterady.*

19th July - *Benjamin Brown and Mary Woodford punished for copying.*

21st July - *Several children absent picking fruit. Charles Orchard attends very irregularly of late and never asks leave.*

27th July - *Kate White punished for obstinacy. She has not appeared this afternoon.* By the beginning of August there are references to children not attending due to the harvest, and Martha Brown seems to have lost some interest in the Log Book, and nothing is recorded until

12th September - *The new master commenced duties* and clearly took a great deal of interest in the school work. The Rector attends quite often, and Scripture Lessons are referred to, but dictation seems to be getting worse! On 15th September 1870 - *I. White and R. White being very carelefs. H. Jenkins away with leave from Master.*

The tone of the Log Book seems to have changed a little, with the new Master clearly taking a great deal of interest in the Scriptures, and arithmetic. The Rector, and Mrs Theobald, regularly attend, Mrs Theobald *examined the slates.*

26th September - *The children spoken to about their behaviour in Church on Sunday.*

24th October - *Fred Lowe absent without leave; reproved.*

27th October - *Several away owing to the Sale of the remains of the wrecked Brig.* (Brigantine - a sailing vessel)

4th November - *Dorcas meeting. Elder children went.*

17th November - *Two strange ladies visited in the afternoon (!). The Atherfield children let out at 3.30 owing to the long distance they have to go.*

The new Master has clearly taken an interest in the Log Book and is insisting on an entry every day, to a point that, to satisfy the rule, on 25th November 1870 - *Nothing of any importance.*

30th November - *A boy punished with cane for mistakes in spelling.*

1871 opens with a return to school on 9th January, and the usual routine dominates the entries for want of something better to say. There are references to *Clara Merritt, Rose Butcher and Harriet Godden 'again'* all being shown absent without leave.

26th January - *Several boys punished for negligence.*

30th January - *Janet Munt leave of absence for week.*

2nd February - *The Upper Grade kept in till 12.35 for inattention*

13th March - *Henry Jenkins reproved for playing before his class.*

28th March - *John, Ellen, and Emily Lowe left for Cowes, fit for Exam.*

29th March - *The whole School exhorted to attend regularly and punctually.*

3rd April - *The commencement of our School Year under the New Education Act of 1871.*

10th March - *Several children away owing to having no shoes.*

The build-up to the 'Inspection' was recorded, and then on 20th April 1871 - *Inspection by H.M.I. T.W. Danby.* Martha records - *I put this to know where it was.* (!)

From this time the way the Log is written changes again, from a daily entry, to a weekly summary of important events, with sub-headings. There is clearly a reorganisation in the teaching of classes.

In the week ended 6th May - *The family of Robert, George, William, and Isabella White from Atherfield Station gave notice of withdrawal as their parents were going to live in Ryde. Caroline Stallard of Appleford also gave notice as she was going to work in the fields. Richard Brown also left to go to Shanklin to work as a page in a Gentleman's family.* Martha Brown now has to sign each page!

In the week ended 20th May - *Kate Sprake only able to come as Half Timer having to work in Morning at Mrs Thobald's (At the Rectory). Harriett Godden as usual, away, excuse, her Mother gardening. Clara and Georgina Merritt taken off the register owing to irregular attendance. Sebastian Bastiani and Robert Sprake* (a future good class of Smuggler!) *monitors this week. William Stephens from Atherfield Coast Guard Station admitted this week at two pence per week.* (Children are now having to make a contribution to their education).

In the week ended 27th May - *Many children absent with Scarletina. Several children reproved for getting into grass fields. Robert Sprake and Edward Mew monitors this week. Robert Sprake keeps good order with his clafs. The cane was not required.*

In the week ended 24th June - *The little Wheelers readmitted having left the Parish while their house was being built. The Master had occasion to punish several this week for bad behaviour in Church. Some Lady visitors called and enquired for Mr Baker who is dead. Arithmetic was not so well done as it ought considering the time spent with Standard by Master. The whole Standard kept in during play-time in order to learn their Multiplication tables.*

In the week ended 8th July - *The beginning of the School quarter, all children to pay their pence quarterly in advance, and during the week nearly all the children in the Masters rooms had paid 1/- in advance for ensuing quarter. Henry Jenkins given 3 weeks of absence in order to fill the place of Rev. Berwick's Groom.*

In the week ended 15th July - *There are a few children whose parents could not possibly pay quarterly, consequently they are permitted to pay weekly as before. William Stephens a boy from Atherfield Coast Guard Station admitted on payment of 2d per week on trial.*

In the week ended 22nd July - *William Stephens absent the whole week in consequence of the death of his sister from Consumption. Daniel King from Atherfield Station absent having gone to work for a few weeks.*

In the week ended 29th July - *Janet Squibb kept at home while her mother went out to look after Mr W. Jacobs. Henry Squibb one of the most troublesome boys in the School was punished several times.*

In the week ended 5th August - *Eliza Kelly who had only recently been admitted after long absence has been away this last fortnight. Harriett King and Janet Squibb ill. Dictation was done well this week and this subject appears to be done very fairly indeed. Sophia Hookey who generally had a large number of mistakes did hers with only two or three.*

In the week ended 12th August - *Robert Rayner and L. Chiverton were absent without permission. Wednesday was a Dorcas Meeting which obliged the School to be differently arranged.*

In the week ended 19th August - *The Rev. Theobald visited the School and advised Master to break up for the Harvest Vacation upon the Master expressing a wish to do so. On Thursday the school broke up, and the Master gave the children a tea on the Friday.*

The School was reopened on Monday, 18th September 1871 *but there were so very few children there that the Rev. Theobald and Master thought it advisable to extend the vacation as the gleaning was not yet completed on one or two farms.* The school reopened again on Monday 25th September but the attendance was little improved. *The Master gave the Upper Standard their first knowledge of the Metric System.*

In the week ended 7th October - *Attendance still poor and on enquiring the Master finds that some had not finished their gleaning yet. The children learned a singing piece called "Oh call my brother back to me'. Friday afternoon there was the Dorcas meeting.*

The week ended 14th October - (under the heading - Case of collission with Squibb's mother) *Two boys F & Henry Squibb were kept in by Master. Their Mother came for them and Master informed her that if she took them away against his orders she must take them for good. The woman was in a passion and took them, well next morning she sent them but I sent them back saying that I could not admit them unlefs the Mother came also and begged my pardon with a promise to submit to the rules of the Master, which was done by her. The Rector was acquainted with the case the next day.*

In the week ended 18th November - *Dictation was better done. I taught Multiplication by 3 this week. Their knowledge of subtraction seems better than last week. New music piece 'If I were a Sunbeam'.*

In the week ended 25th November - *The Fever broke out in the Parish in consequence of which Janet Sprake and Walter Sprake were obliged to stay at home as their sister had it, then Walter and Janet got it and were some time getting over it. There are several girls and boys ill with colds, but I do not hear of the Fever being anywhere else but Sprakes at present. There was a holiday on 8th, Kingston Church being reopened on that day, and Master having occasion to go and lead the singing, the children had a holiday.*

In the week ended 16th December - *Two more cases of Fever, Clara and Alice Chiverton of Newman Lane. The attendance was not so good, so many have colds and parents are afraid to send them to School. Elizabeth Hendy taken ill and was obliged to keep her bed, taken very ill in School was obliged to be sent home. Janet Squibb also taken ill and was sent home.*

In the week ended 25th December - *General Examination in the subject of Reading, Writing, and Arithmetic showed that most of the children appeared to know their work, but there was a want of accuracy in Arithmetic generally. Edward Mew did his very well indeed. The spelling too was on the whole an improvement. The School broke up on 24th December for Xmas Vacation.*

1872 In the week ended 13th January - *Emily Spanner and Rose Hendy have the Hooping Cough, and the family of Chivertons the fever.*

In the week ended 21st January - *The Hooping Cough is getting very much spread in this Parish. Consequently many absent; about 15 cases in the Parish. On Tuesday two boys played Truant (Followed the Hounds) they begged Masters pardon on Wednesday and as it is a rare occurance they were not severely punished.*

In the week ended 24th February - *Several absent - Harriett King owing to the illness of her Mother. W. Brown and R. Creeth absent from no cause given. Edward Mew as usual did his work remarkably well and was commended by the Rector.*

In the week ended 16th March - *Henry Bushell obliged to be sent home being taken ill with a sick headache. Janet Sprake also sent home exhibiting signs of Hooping Cough. Master absent all week with an attack of the chest. The Rector took the classes and the Master submitted the general work.*

In the week ended 6th April - *There was no Easter Holidays this week owing to the Examinations, the children readily consented to have their holidays some future time. Harriett Godden away nearly all week, reason illness.*

In the week ended 18th May - *Spelling lesson - several found not able to spell the word 'against'. Mary Thorn and Janet Munt given leave of absence for a fortnight to visit their friends. Several away helping friends and parents hay making.*

In the week ended 15th June - *Several attended very irregularly indeed. Roland Creeth, Charles Orchard, Walter Brown, and Charles Kent at times - they have been spoken to strongly upon the subject. Clara, Janet and Alice Chiverton absent again having the Measles badly.*

In the week ended 20th July - *Florence Lowe absent though illness. Some lady visitors from Ventnor visited the School in the afternoon, just looked round, passed no comment. The whole school kept in till 5 o'clock on Thursday evening owing to the noise coming in from recreation. Still there are several absent who might be at School, but the parents are very indifferent in the matter.*

School broke up for Harvest Vacation on 10th August 1872.

In the week ended 14th September - *The school reopened after the Harvest Vacation with a small attendance, many children still gleaning, several farms not having carried all the wheat, which kept those whose fathers worked on that from school - several were ill.*

In the week ended 30th November - *Charles Orchard sent home for school money - his mother having questioned its being owing. Minnie Wheeler gone to Ventnor as her Mother is ill.*

By December a number of children had left the school for various reasons.

In the week ended 21st December - *Attendance not good until Friday morning when nearly all were present no doubt owing to the <u>Bread</u> being given away.* Then the school broke up for Christmas.

1873 In the week ended 18th January - *The school reopened after the Xmas vacation with a very poor attendance. The great reason for being absent upon enquiry being that they had no boots to wear. Master spoke to one parent about her 3 children and she stated that she really wanted them to come but they had no shoes, and she could not send them. The Atherfield children have not attended since the vacation - fears are entertained that they have been enticed to attend Shorwell. On Thursday morning it was snowing consequently there was very thin attendance.*

A page from Chale School s Log Book - 1873

NAME.	ADMISSION.							OCCUPATION OF PARENTS.
	Index No.	Date of Admission.	Age. Yrs.	Age. Mos.	Class.	How long in any other School?	In what Standard examined in last School?	
Mew Emily	94	8.5.76	5	0				Thatcher
Chiverton Ellen	95	29.5.76	3	9				Coast Guard
Linington William	96	15.5.76	5	4				Blacksmith
Howell William	97	19.6.76	4	8				Coast Guard
Sprake Percy	98	18.9.76	3	7				Dead
Nutson Sarah Ann	99	8.1.76	3	0				Diver
Hardy Mary	100	22.1.76	3	0				Labourer
Stallard Charles	101	2.4.77	4	9				Carpenter
Cheek Alice Kake	102	9.4.77	4	1				Hurdle maker
Lowe Minnie	103	30.4.77	4	10				Shoemaker
Weeks George	104	7.5.77	5	5				Labourer
Gosden Fredrick	105	8.5.77	3	11				Labourer
Reynolds George	106	28.5.77	4	7				Labourer
Sprake Frank	107	28.5.77	3	7	—			Labourer
Chiverton Henry	108	28.5.77	4	9				Labourer
Buckell William	109	4.6.77	3	0				Dead
Chiverton Herbert	110	11.6.77	3	5				Carrier
Sturmey Annie	111	11.6.77	4	11				Labourer
Janes Henry William	112	18.6.77	4	10				Coast Guard
Andrews Matilda Rosina	113	24.9.77	3	2				Coast Guard
Coleman Lousia	114	26.11.77	4	6				Labourer
Pengelly J. William	115	7.1.78	5	10				Coast Guard
Butcher Thomas	116	7.1.78	3	0				Labourer
Butcher Walter	117	15.4.78	5	1	—			Labourer
Cotton Frank	118	15.4.78	3	7				Farmer
Coombes Eva	119	15.4.78	4	0	+			Baker
Jacobs Henry	120	1.5.78	5	1				Dead
Pomery William	121	6.5.78	4	0				Keeper
Linington Sidney	122	13.5.78	5	0	—			Black-smith
Cheek Fredrick	123	13.5.78	4	1	+			Shepherd
Hoyles Rose Jane	124	14.5.78	4	11	—			Dead
Trent George	125	14.5.78	4	1	+			Labourer

The Log Book ends abruptly at this point, save for the start of a short story. But, on February 21st 1894, the Organizing Visitor's Report on Chale Infants School is given -

"The Reading continues highly satisfactory. Counting is good, & Writing is excellent. All the work is conscientiously and successfully performed, the tone of the School is cheerful and bright, and teaching keeps well abreast of modern requirements"

Signed. A. Munday, March 7th 1894

Not a bad situation for a small village school. The Rector clearly took a close and active role in the lessons, particularly in scripture, and visited the school every week.

As well as the Log Book, Martha kept numerous attendance records, and the Admission Register for the Infants School from 1870 to 1893. It is interesting to note that children were starting school (according to the entries) as young as 2 years, (although that may have been anything up to 3 years), and 3 years was quite common. The 'parents' (presumably the father) occupation at admission was recorded, and included

Harriett Bastiani (aged 3) - parent Fisherman, of Chale;
Rosina Woodford - Sawyer, of Chale Green;
Mary Cheek - Dairyman, of Pyle;
Annie Snudden - Coast Guard, of Atherfield Station;
Frederick Butcher - Shepherd, of Oxford (presumably 'Oxford Dairy');
Daniel Morris - Farmer, of North Grounds;
Emily New - Thatcher; of South-down;
Minnie Lowe - Shoemaker, of Chale Green;
Alice Cheek - Hurdlemaker of Chale;
Eva Coombes - Baker, of Chale;
Ernest Chiverton - Carrier, of Black-gang;
Arthur Abbott - Hostler, of Black-gang;
and members of the Sprake family - Brewer, of Town Lane.

But a lot of children had parents who are described as 'Dead', an indication of how many people died at an early age in those times and how many children grew up never knowing one or both parents.

Martha Brown gained a Teachers Certificate of the Third Class in 1872, issued by The Lords of the Committee of the Privy Council on Education, and written on velum. Teachers in the Third Class were not recognised for the superintendence of Pupil Teachers until they had risen to a higher class by examination. Martha Brown was awarded her certificate 'without examination' having been a 'Teacher of Elementary Schools for more than 10 years'. This entitled her to teach infants only up to the age of 7 years.

Her certificate contained a report on her practical skill - *"M.Brown possesses many qualifications for an Infant School Mistress; her mode of teaching is firm, yet kind, and she has had considerable experience"*.

Regular reports on inspection of Martha Brown's work was endorsed on the Certificate every year around the end of April or early May from 1873 to 1890. These include -

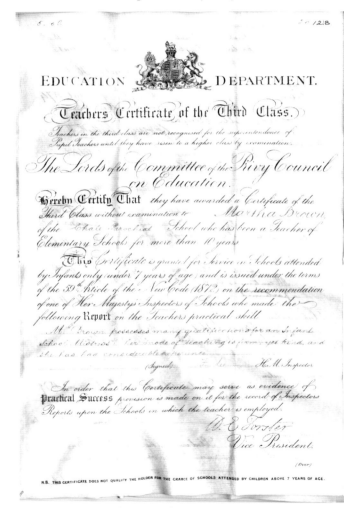

Martha Brown's Teachers Certificate 1872

"The infants department has been very efficiently conducted during the past year"; 1873

"The Infants are very carefully and successfully taught"; 1874

"All going on well"; 1875

"This department continues to be carried on pleasantly and successfully"; 1876

"All continues to be satisfactory in the Infants department"; 1877

"The infants have been well taught"; 1878

"The infants are in good order, & make very fair and satisfactory progress"; 1881

"This school continues to do well"; 1883

"A well taught school in excellent discipline"; 1884

"The infants are taught with care and success"; 1886

"This is in all points a praiseworthy school"; 1887

"The instruction of the infants deserved praise"; 1888

"The infants are kindly and suitably taught by Miss Brown"; 1890

A Report of Religious Instruction in Chale Infants School, dated 23rd May 1898, states that The Old Testament, the New Testament, and Repetition were all *"Very Good"*; and general remarks included *"Great pains has been spent upon religious instruction of these children with thoroughly good results. The children are being well trained in habits of reverence and order, and a valuable religious work is being done"*.

The Report for 1900 only gave *"Good"* for the three catagories, and the General Remarks state *"The school continues to do a good and useful religious work. The children are being brought up to be reverent, and interested in their subject. Their knowledge has somewhat suffered this year through the closing of the School during several weeks. A good syllabus has been taught"*.

All in all, Martha Brown appears to have been a very caring and successful teacher, no doubt much loved by her young charges.

In October 1903 she made a contribution of 18/4d under the Elementary School Teachers Superannuation Act 1898, being a contribution to the Deferred Annuity Fund for the period from 1st May to 30th September 1903.

Martha Brown retired from the School in 1904 at the age of 65 years,

A Chale School Concert c. 1890 (Martha Brown at back; John Cook (Master) in centre)

and died at the end of that year, in her little home which is still known to this day as 'Martha Brown's House'. Chale Infants School was her life, and she died unmarried, probably of a broken heart at having to give up her teaching. Maybe she did not have any children of her own, but she looked after hundreds of children in her dedicated life as the Infants Teacher.

School accounts 1894 & 1895

The accounts for the 'Chale Parochial Schools' for the year to 30th April in each of these years reveal that it cost around £230 a year to run the two schools. The major cost was the teachers salaries, totalling some £160 per year, including £116 for the 'teachers'; £40 for the Assistant Mistress; and £7.6.8d for an Articled Pupil Teacher. Books, apparatus, and stationery amounted to some £18 per year. Each year there was an item of £1.1/- shown as 'Organising Master'; clearly he needed little organising!

On the income side, a government grant of some £90 p.a. was received; fee grants produced some £50 yearly; and there were 'endowments' of £22.15.0d annually. But some £45 was received each year from subscriptions, mainly from local people. Lady Mary Gordon gave £5, and the Rector, Rev.C.W. Heald (who was also the Treasurer) gave £7 each year. 14/6 was received each year from the 'Admiralty'; and £1.10/- from the 'Guardians of the Isle of Wight'. Tom Roberts contributed £1 each year; and Messrs and Miss Sprake, and Mr Spanner, 7/6d each annually. Clearly the local community took much pride in supporting their local school.

However, in the days when the OFSTED and other inspections are awaited with some trepidation, it may be interesting to note that in the 1890's, the annual visit by H.M. Inspector's was probably equally feared. In his published report as part of the accounts for 1894 the following comments are seen:-

Mixed School - *"Tone, Drill, and Discipline deserves praise. Instruction is zealous and intelligent, and the results are satisfactory, allowance being made for serious hindrances. Attainments in the 1st and 2nd Standards, and Needlework in all Standards are very creditable points. History is good, and geography fair. The Premises and Offices have been much improved and enlarged. The Fencing of the Playground should be completed as soon as possible".*

Infants' School - *"The state of the Infants School continues to be good. A. Sprake has passed fairly. Drawing - Good"*

The Report for 1895 is in similar vein. -

Mixed School - *"Tone, discipline and drill deserve very high praise. Instruction is zealous and intelligent. Reading throughout the school, and the attainments of the younger children are good points. Arithmetic in the higher standards has suffered from serious hindrances. History is satisfactory, Geography and Needlework excellent. Singing by note shows great progress".*

Infants' school - *"The Infants School steadily maintains its creditable character. A.Sprake has passed fairly. Drawing "Good"*

The rather bland comment on 'A.Sprake' refers to Miss Arabella Sprake (sister of Octavia Sprake who later married Henry Roberts) who was a 'Pupil Teacher'. I am not sure if 'passed fairly' is praise or not!

Reference in the 1894 accounts to the improvement and enlargement of the premises are covered in a separate Statement of Accounts. The costs of the work came to £219.16.3d. Income came from legacies and grants, including £20 from the Winchester Diocesan Board of Education, and £5 from 'an Island Rector'. The Rev and the Misses Nutter held a concert and donated £5.10/- (all expenses being paid by them). However, the main materials were all donated - stone by Lady Mary Gordon; lime by Mr Way of Pyle; sand by Mr Charles Dabell; and cartage by Messrs Jolliffe, Way, Morris, Russell, Spanner and Sprake - the value of these services was stated as £70.00. Once again, the local community made a substantial contribution in kind to their School.

The Treasurer and Managers of the School recorded their gratitude for the generous donations; and the 'munificent grants' from the Diocesan and National Society's.

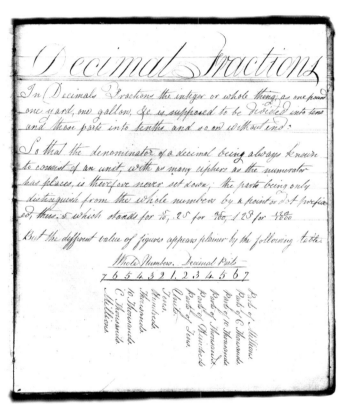

A page from Charles Sprake's Chale Schools Arithmetic book - 1859 (Aged 13 years)

It may be of interest to those children at Chale School today who look through their playground railings at the passing traffic that these railings were erected over 100 years ago. 'What the Victorian's did for us!!'

In 1929, the school accounts reveal a bequest from the late Alfred Spanner of £500 for 'the purchase of the playground and erection of shelters' (which were a feature of the playground until the new school hall and kitchens were built). The cost of the land for the playground was just £50, and understood to have been purchased from Tom Roberts. The shelters were built a little later and no cost is recorded. By 1929 the only ordinary expenses met by the School Accounts was £4.10/- for cleaning and £2.3.3d. for Oil and fuel! Fred Mew was the Treasurer, and Henry Roberts, Auditor. The Roberts family still had an important role in the school administration.

As a footnote, I feel I must mention the 'dare' for younger boys in years long past, which was to crawl up the drain pipe from the road outside the school to near the outside toilets at the top of the playground; something which I could never have attempted. But many did. I am told that the pipe got quite narrow in the centre and it was quite a squeeze for some to get through. I have heard of blocked drains, but that was one venture too far!

Chale School 1904 - Back row from left, 2nd Arthur Sprake, 3rd Octavia Sprake, 5th Elsie Sprake.
Middle row from left, 3rd Tom Sprake.

CHAPTER 4

THE CLARENDON HOTEL, AND TOM & GRACE ROBERTS

Whilst at the start of the 21st century, the visitor to Chale will be familiar with the name, 'The Wight Mouse', to those who have lived in the village for a number of years, the name will forever be 'The Clarendon'. The importance and reputation of this establishment in the first half of the 1900's was due entirely to Tom and Grace Roberts; during their occupation it attracted the famous (and no doubt, infamous); Royalty; the titled; and some who transformed the course of history.

Tom and Grace Roberts were 'The Clarendon Hotel', and their influence on Chale and the people who lived and worked there, and who played there, was immense. They were Chale!

Tom Roberts mother, Mary Brown, who had married Thomas Pinnock Roberts, and who was left a widow when her husband failed to return home from the United States of America, brought up her only son in the cottage next to the village blacksmith's shop, a stones throw away

The Clarendon Hotel 1899

from The Clarendon Hotel. Little is known of his childhood, but he was educated in the village school opposite his home, and where his Aunt, Martha Brown was the Infants Mistress. Farming and horses were his life, and he earned a living from both. On leaving school he started work as a guard on Dabell's Coach at Blackgang, and then became a Carrier, travelling between Chale and Newport, taking over from another well-known local resident, Maurice Rayner. This brought him in contact with most of the local population, collecting and delivering parcels; doing shopping for his customers; and taking passengers into the Market Town of Newport.

SEASON 1890.

"PRINCE,"

A well-bred red roan Hackney Horse, 15hds.3ins., the property of T. Roberts, Chale, and formerly belonging to Mr. Monkton, Grange Farm, Wimborne,

Will travel the Island this Season and stand at the Green Dragon Stables, Newport, on Market Days.

Fees, 35s. inclusive. The groom's fee, 5s., to be paid the first time of serving, and the remainder at the time of foaling.

All letters and orders to be sent to

T. ROBERTS, Chale

Tom Roberts owned and bred horses, and provided a Hackney Taxi service for the local gentry, a trade which he continued for many years, incorporating it with The Clarendon Hotel trade. By 1890 Tom had a stallion standing at stud by the name of 'Prince'. In those days the horse was the sole provider of transport, and the need to breed sound replacement stock was paramount for any business. A printed card, as can be seen, provided details for his prospective customers. Prince had been brought to the Island to improve the stock here, and could be seen by those who were interested at The Green Dragon Stables, at the Pyle Street end of Town Lane in Newport, on Market Days - the one day of the week when all farmers would meet in nearby St James Square (still known by older residents as 'The Market').

In 1891, changes were afoot in Chale. Both the local village shop and bakery, opposite the Church, and The Clarendon Hotel, next to the Church and on the other side of the road from the shop, were up for 'sale'. Walter Brown (no relation of the 'Blacksmith Brown's', Tom Roberts family), who also had a Carriers business, had his eye on the Hotel; Tom had his on the shop, and by all accounts each was about to take over these businesses. But chance would have it that the reverse actually happened. Walter Brown, whose brother John Brown was also to run the village shop on the Green at Chale, took over the shop and bakery, and Tom Roberts got the Hotel!

There may have been a less obvious reason for this, and that was all because of love! In 1859, Grace Senior was born in Yorkshire, the daughter of Joseph Senior, a Blanket Weaver, whose father was a publican, James Senior of Earls Heaton. Joseph also spent time in the licence trade. No doubt this upbringing was to have an influence on her future involvement in the Chale hotel. As was often the case in Victorian times, young Grace went into service at the age of just 12 years with Canon W. Heald, the Vicar of Birstall in Yorkshire, to be the companion to his daughter Harriet. Grace was to remain with Harriet until her marriage.

It was this situation which brought Grace to Chale on the Isle of Wight. Harriet Heald married a priest, the Rev. William Rhodes. Grace Senior stayed with her now married companion and moved with the Rhodes family, and when the Rev. Rhodes was appointed Rector of Chale in 1884, Grace Senior came to Chale also. Sadly, the Rev. Rhodes died soon afterwards, at the young age of 36 years whilst in office at Chale. The vacant living was taken over by Harriet Rhodes brother, the Rev. Charles Heald, with whom his sister continued to reside in Chale Rectory until her death in 1924. Charles Heald was to have a remarkable influence on his parish and became a highly respected and much loved Rector.

Joseph Senior and grandsons - Henry (standing) and Ridley Roberts c. 1899.

Life in a village Rectory in late Victorian times was almost a community in itself, and at various times other members of Grace Senior's family were welcomed into the fold. Her sister, and her brother James Senior resided there from time to time, as did Charles Heald's brother John, who was also a Clerk in Holy Orders. James Senior was a particularly close member of the Senior family, and was to serve with distinction throughout the Great War, and was to die in German hands.

We can only surmise how Grace Senior and Tom Roberts met, but meet they did, and in 1892 they married. As has been mentioned, at the time of the impending wedding, the two businesses at the upper end of the village became available. Grace had had connections with the licensed trade and would have had some knowledge of it, and during her time living in Chale Rectory she had undertaken the role of Cook to the family. I must assume that this background had some influence on why they took over the licence of The Clarendon Hotel, and became Managers there, and not the shop. Even her brother, James Senior, was involved as a Domestic Servant and Waiter from the age of 14 years, although on marriage he lived in London. A very close association between the Roberts family and Chale Church was established, which lasted through to Tom and Grace's grandson, Edward Roberts death, in 2004. It was Chale Church which brought them together.

But God works in mysterious ways! The village of Chale and its residents have prospered from the sea for centuries; from fishing, mainly for Mackerel; from the fruits of the Cross Channel Trade (Smuggling); and from the fortuitous arrival in the Bay of the occasional ship which foundered on the shore. Not that the locals wanted the events to cause the loss of life which it so often did, but for the rewards it brought in salvaged cargo or the timbers of the ships. Many of those who lived by the sea served in the rescue service and became crew members of the lifeboats which were stationed along the Back of the Wight at Brooke, Brighstone, and Atherfield. But once the lives were saved, a good wreck served the community well.

In the early part of the 19th century, Casey's Cottage stood on the site near the Church, and a small ale house known as The White Mouse was established nearby. Around 1845 a larger house was built probably joining the two buildings, to form an hotel with its public bar.

On the morning of 11th October 1836, the ship 'Clarendon' laden with Rum, Sugar, etc., travelling from St. Kitts and bound for London foundered below Blackgang Chine. Rare at that time, there were women and children on board the vessel, and it was their sad deaths in the severe storm, and the sight of their bodies strewn on the shore which sickened all who were present. 18 of the crew and passengers were buried in Chale Churchyard between 13th and 15th October 1836. The ships timbers were salvaged, and most were sold to construct what was to be known as The Clarendon, at Shanklin, which was being built at the time. No doubt some were used locally, and some parts were kept; part of the keel being stored at the home of Tom Roberts and his family for nearly 150 years.

This tragic event led to the building of St. Catherines Lighthouse at Niton, in an effort to provide better warning for passing ships of the dangers of Chale Bay and the rocks at Rocken End. The area is particularly dangerous due to a deep trench, or trough (always referred to as 'The Trow' by locals) some yards off shore all along the western coast of the Isle of Wight, which would trap any vessel whose keel should happen to drop within its depth. Once in the trow, never to escape. To commemorate the wreck and its victims, the White Mouse was re-named The Clarendon only to be erroneously changed to The Wight Mouse some 150 years later. But it will always be 'The Clarendon' to Chalers.

In January 1892 Grace Senior married Tom Roberts in Chale Church, the service being conducted by the Rev. Charles Heald, and Grace being given away by her long-time companion and the Rectors sister, Harriet Rhodes. She wore a cinnamon coloured velvet dress (white wedding dresses were rarely used then), and a wedding breakfast was held in the Rectory where Mrs Rhodes had prepared a magnificent cake. In the evening a reception was held in The Clarendon with about 50 guests. One present, from the Rectory, was a silver sugar basin, sugar tongs, and cream jug in a case, which has been passed down through the Roberts family, to this day.

On their marriage, when Tom and Grace took over as Managers of The Clarendon Hotel, fortune shone on Chale once again with the memorable wreck of the s.s. Eider. Shortly before the event, a new lifeboat had been stationed at Atherfield, called the 'Catherine Swift', after the benefactor of that name who lived at Lowcliffe House at the seaward end of the Terrace. On the night of 31st January 1892 the North German steamer 'Eider' of 4,719 tons, ran aground on Atherfield Ledge. She had 227 passengers in addition to the crew; and carried 500 sacks of mail and some £300,000 worth of gold and silver ingots. The three local lifeboats, including the new 'Catherine Swift', whose crew included Walter

'Catherine Swift', Atherfield Lifeboat, and crew - 1891.

Woodford who later lived at Denhams next to the Roberts, performed a remarkable rescue, and all were saved, and all the bullion on board was also brought ashore by the lifeboats and carted away under armed guard. Many of those rescued were taken to The Clarendon where Tom and Grace Roberts gladly entertained them; the rescued and the rescuers literally consumed all available food from both the Hotel and the village shop. Trade was good, and over the ensuing years, they were fortunate to provide food and shelter for those involved in many wrecks in Chale Bay. As letters sent and recorded here later reveal, the news of a ship ashore was greated with some joy!

In the mid 1800's, such as Fanny and Hilary Dabell, and later Jeremiah Lowe (who played the Bassoon in the Church orchestra before an organ was built there) ran the establishment. When the Roberts took over The Clarendon in 1892, the property was owned by the Trustees of Frank Barton, leased to the Newport Brewers, W.B. Mew Langton & Co. Ltd, The Royal Brewers who had appointed a Manager to run it, and Eliza Elliott held the Licence. Tom and Grace Roberts became their Managers, and Tom held the Licence. When later, in 1901, the property was sold, it was bought by Mew Langton's, and the Robert's were granted a 21 year Lease, which was later renewed and continued until after the death of Tom in 1943. Their future in the Hotel was now secure.

Business was sound, and the Hotel attracted a good trade. A receipt dated May 1896 shows a monthly purchase of wine, spirits and ale from the brewers of £32. Tom was able to expand, not only the hotel and bar trade, but his taxi service which was widely used by the local hierarchy, and for weddings all over the Island. A Publican's Licence authorised them to sell spirits, wine, sweets, made wines, mead, metheglin, beer, cider and perry; also to deal in and sell tobacco and snuff. The duties payable around 1900 being £20.00 as a retailer of spirits, and 5/3d as a dealer in tobacco. By 1915, the duties had increased to £27.10/- for spirits, but the tobacco duty was still 5/3d.

A licence was required to operate with Hackney Carriages, and in 1908 Tom Roberts had a license to operate seven carriages, at 15/- each, a total cost per annum of £5.5/-. It was an expensive business, but the trade must have justified the cost, and the need to have seven carriages at the ready was an indication of the number of wealthy residents in the area at that time.

Tom and Grace Roberts were not rich! As was common at that time, the wealthy gentry of the district often provided those in business with loans, rather than them going to a Bank or other lender. These institutions would usually require security in the form of a charge (a mortgage) over property, and Tom did not own any at that time. The local squire would provide. And so it was that, from the evidence of the many receipts and loan notes still to hand, it was to this source that the Roberts turned to run and expand their businesses. By the similarly numerous receipts, they always honoured their commitments.

Evidence of the lack of funds, or perhaps their reluctance to spend money on other peoples property, were the numerous letters between the brewery landlords and their tenants seeking urgent repairs and refurbishment to the hotel, mainly it would seem, met with some reluctance on the part of Mew Langtons!

Many will remember the Monkey Puzzle Tree which stood outside the Hotel; planted by Tom on his arrival there in 1892, to eventually die in the 1970's.

Henry Roberts at Chale School 1906 (left, second row from back)

The reputation of The Clarendon Hotel at Chale attracted the custom of many wealthy people, including Royalty. Princess Beatrice, youngest daughter of Queen Victoria stayed there before the Great War, as did the King and Queen of Spain (the daughter of Princess Beatrice, Princess Eugenie, also known as Princess Ena; and when Queen, Queen Victoria of Spain; and King Alfonso), who

stayed there twice. A rare photograph shows Her Majesty leaving the Hotel with her Lady-in-Waiting. In a letter written to Tom and Grace's sons in November 1908, there is a comment that "..you all had a gay time during the King of Spain's visit; I should have liked to have been there very much...", clearly referring to the close relationship between them and their royal visitors. How proud the Roberts were to attract such elite clientele. Their custom brought many to stay in the establishment in the ensuing years.

Her Majesty the Queen of Spain leaving The Clarendon Hotel

Alexander Fleming stayed at The Clarendon Hotel in the 1920's, and whilst there noticed the fine growth of mould on the top of the pig-swill tub. All waste food was deposited here and boiled up for the pigs to eat, but was rarely emptied. At the time Fleming was experimenting with such things, and gained permission from Tom Roberts to take a sample of the Clarendon 'mould' back to Scotland with him. He later discovered 'Penicillin' (using the 'mould' in his experiments), which changed medical history; who knows, without Chale it may never have been discovered!

AN ACCOUNT of the Money collected and spent on the
Restoration of the Bells of Chale Parish Church.

RECEIPTS.		£	s.	d.		EXPENDITURE.		£	s.	d.
1895-7.					1896.					
To Subscriptions, Proceeds of Concerts, Sale of Work, etc.:—					Dec. 12	Messrs. Creeth, new Floor to Belfry, as per Estimate		8	17	0
George A. Hearn, Esq., of New York	...	10	0	0	,, 17	Mr. Brown, Mason's Work in Tower in connection with fixing				
Captain Killick's Entertainment	...	8	6	0		Bells		1	0	6
,, Casberd-Boteler	...	1	1	0						
J. H. Paul, Esq., M.D.	...	16	19	0	1897.					
Captain Killick's Lecture	...	1	4	0	March 18	Messrs. Taylor's Account, including re-casting cracked bell,				
Mr. Cooke's Concert (net)	...	2	0	0		repair to small bell, new bell, new fittings for three bells,				
Miss D. Casberd-Boteler	...	1	0	0		and framework for four bells (less discount at 2 per cent.)	118	15	8
,, M. Casberd-Boteler	...	1	0	0		Carriage to and from Works		8	4	8
,, Jolliffe's Concert	...	5	10	0		Winchester Registrar for Faculty		1	12	0
Mrs. Butterfield	...	10	0	0						
Miss Fairclough	...	1	0	0						
Mrs. Theobald, Mrs. Collet, and Lady Stamford	...	2	10	0						
Ven. Archdeacon Haigh	...	1	0	0						
Rev. J. Bailey, Rural Dean	...	1	1	0						
Lee, Esq., London	...	1	1	0						
Messrs. Sprake	...	10	0							
Mrs. Harvey, of Marvel	...	1	0	0						
Mr. A. Spanner	...	1	0	0						
Sale of Work (net)	...	50	0	9						
R. Pinnock, Esq.	...	1	1	0						
Mrs. Heald	...	5	0	0		C. W. HEALD, Rector.				
Rev. J. M. Heald	...	5	0	0		J. D. JOLLIFFE, } Churchwardens.				
,, C. W. Heald	...	5	0	0		HENRY WAY, }				
Sale of articles left from Sale of Work	...	8	9	5						
Churchwardens' grant from Church box for Fee for Registrar of						Dated March 21st, 1897.				
Winchester	...	1	12	0						
Miss Jolliffe's Concert	...	2	17	6						
Rev. R. Leslie Morris	...	1	1	0						
Hy. Way, Esq., Pyle	...	5	0	0		By Credit Balance	...	1	9	10
		£139	19	8				£139	19	8

SERVICE
FOR THE
Dedication of Bells,
OF
CHALE CHURCH,
ON
✳ SEPTEMBER 9th, 1897. ✳

HYMN 166.—"All people that on earth do dwell."
The Archdeacon will deliver an Address.

Our Father, &c., *Amen.*
V. Sing we merrily unto God our Strength.
R. Make a cheerful noise unto the God of Jacob.
V. O GOD, make speed to save us.
R. O Lord make haste to help us.
V. Glory be to the FATHER, and to the SON, and to the HOLY GHOST.
R. As it was in the beginning, is now, and ever shall be, world without end. Amen.
V. Praise ye the LORD.
R. The Lord's name be praised.

PSALM CL.

V. Every one that did offer an offering of silver and brass.
R. Brought the Lord's offering.
V. They offered them before the LORD.
R. Therefore they are hallowed.
V. Our help is in the name of the LORD;
R. Who hath made Heaven and earth.
V. Blessed be the name of the LORD.
R. Who hath made Heaven and earth.

Chale Church was ever close to the Roberts' hearts, and they took every opportunity to encourage others to support its needs. A regular visitor to the hotel was Mr G. Hearn of New York and he provided several stained glass windows, the organ, and the church clock, all at Tom Roberts' suggestion. In the 1930's, Count Michel Karolyi (the first President of Hungary) and his family stayed at The Clarendon regularly whilst in exile from his Country, and was eventually buried in the Churchyard following his death in 1955, as was his son, Adam, following an air accident at Sandown Airport in 1939. Both bodies were later exhumed and returned to Hungary where they received a State funeral.

But this was just part of the Roberts remarkable involvement, and direct influence, in the course of the history of Chale. Tom Roberts was a businessman way ahead of his time, and he was ever open to new ideas to broaden the appeal of his hotel. His clients needed more than just a bed and good food, they needed entertainment. And just as establishments do in more modern times, he looked to sport to attract their trade.

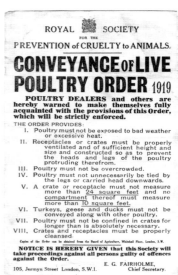

Conveyance of Live Poultry Order 1919

Clarendon Hotel. Chale. Isle of Wight.

Tennis courts were built at the rear of the hotel, in well maintained gardens, overlooking the magnificent views to The Needles, and beyond. These attracted tennis parties which in turn required the provision of 'teas', with spectators sitting on the veranda enjoying home made cakes, and a cup of tea.

Tom Roberts was one of the originators of Chale Golf Club which was established on the Downs overlooking Chale in 1903, with the Club House perched on Gore Cliff (where it still stands to this day as a dwelling off the View Point Car Park, at Blackgang). This also attracted more visitors, and whilst he may not have

Tennis at the Clarendon Hotel c. 1910

"Table" - The Home Hole, Chale Golf Club

helped finance the venture, the existence of a golf course nearby was another feature of his business. The Chale Golf Course had nine holes, but by going round the course twice for a full round, it was an eighteen hole course! Sadly, events outside of their control brought an early end to the venture by 1940, with the major landslide along the Undercliff at Blackgang in 1928 forcing a New Road to be built through the course in the 1930's, and German bombs landing near the course in the Second World War.

CHALE GOLF CLUB.

Competition.....................................

Marked for...   Date...................................192_

	Yards	Bogey	Hole Strokes Allowed.	Player's Score.	Result Won + Lost − Halved 0		Yards	Bogey	Hole Strokes allowed.	Player's Score.	Result Won + Lost − Halved 0
1 Quarry.........	235	4				10 Quarry	235	4			
2 Gore Cliff....	410	5				11 Gore Cliff ...	410	5			
3 Five Rocks...	255	4				12 Five Rocks.	255	4			
4 Chantry	400	6				13 Chantry	400	6			
5 Tolt Rocks ..	382	5				14 Tolt Rocks..	382	5			
6 Old Home ...	230	4				15 Old Home...	230	4			
7 Gulley	195	4				16 Gulley........	195	4			
8 Valley	220	4				17 Valley........	220	4			
9 Table	130	3				18 Table	130	3			
	2457	39					2457	39			

Total 1st Round

Total 2nd   ,,

Gross Score   ...

Handicap   ...

Net   ...   ...

Total Holes +

Total Holes −

Marker.

Result of Match

SIX INCHES.

Ladies Golf tournament c. 1925
Chale Golf Club
left Chale Golf Club - Score Card

The Roberts provided facilities for many official dinners, and the local Scouts, who were formed under the enthusiastic support of the local Head Teacher, John Cooke who resided in the school opposite the hotel and who was a pioneer of scouting in the area, met there for their events. Tom Roberts was no doubt involved in the scouts building their own Scouts Hall (or Hut as it is often known) a short distance from the hotel around 1912. And also the building of the strangely named Chale Conservative Working Mens Club nearby, around the same time, which survives today as the Chale Womens Institute Hall, and is the Village Hall. Tom's son, Henry, as will be seen, was closely involved in its success between the wars when it was the Chale Village Club.

Chale Scout Hut c. 1925

Chale Scouts Parade outside The Clarendon Hotel c. 1925

The Staff of The Clarendon c. 1910. Henry Roberts - centre back row.
Tom Roberts; Ridley Roberts; Grace Roberts front row

Tom also saw the growing need to provide a better water supply for his establishment, and was instrumental in encouraging the provision of a new mains water supply for Chale in the early part of the 20th century, and whilst this would no doubt have come eventually, it brought Chale to the forefront of modern facilities before some other remote country districts, for which we should be ever grateful.

Well satisfied visitors would often send presents and mementoes of their visit, such as the barometer sent by Mr L. Matthews, a London manufacturer of magic lanterns, in 1899.

The Clarendon was not just an hotel, with a public bar; but a taxi business; and a farm. Land, and premises, were usually rented, until over the ensuing years some was purchased, or parts inherited from the Brown family. Every opportunity was taken to purchase and trade, and when the large houses of Lowcliffe and Southlands along the Undercliffe road began to fall victim of the coastal landslides, stone and other building materials were bought on demolition, and stored around the hotel land to be sold on to local builders in later years.

By 1917, when as Grace Roberts' letters will reveal, the hotel was often very busy with both visitors and soldiers, they employed 2 domestic servants, annual wages £92; a gardener, cowman and coachman (presumably Frank Pratt) for £78; a 'boots' and general hand for £52 (£1 per week!); and some casual employees, as well as working themselves. Employers' Liability Insurance for these costing just £1.17.6d. per annum!

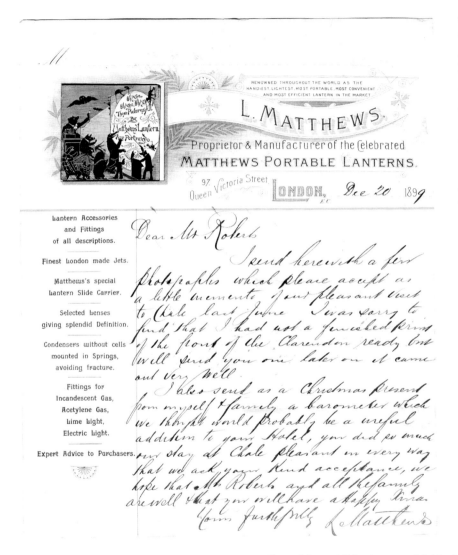

Tom Roberts joined the Parish Council, with particular interest in footpaths, particularly to the shore (no doubt to ensure he had a good access in the event of a wreck, to enable him to recover any fruits of the sea; and also for the use of fishermen). He was well known for many anecdotes about local events, and would recount stories of many trips around the Island. He claimed to have driven horses along almost every road on the Island, and by reputation, in his failing months, would entertain friends around his bed, where carriage reins were attached to the foot of the bedstead, and with a whip in hand, he described journeys along the Island roads.

Grace Roberts died in 1939, and Tom Roberts in 1943, when his son Ridley took over the Licence for a short time until the furniture was eventually sold on 17th August 1944. The hotel remained a Mew's establishment, (until eventually bought out by Strong's), with their familiar Pub Sign depicting a red faced Quaker gentleman with a frothing pint of beer, hung outside the hotel.

Tom and Grace Roberts c. 1935

Grace Roberts

Tom Roberts

CHAPTER 5

A DEAD HERO IS BETTER THAN A LIVE COWARD

When Tom and Grace Roberts' son, Henry, left Chale to join the Royal Engineers late in 1915 he left behind the love of his young life, Ada Octavia Sprake, the eighth and youngest daughter of Oscar Sprake of Sprakes Brewery in Town Lane, Chale. She was always known as Octavia or 'Tave', (unless she was angry about something, when she called herself Ada!).

Not only had Henry joined the British Army, but he had moved to train in Wales, which for Octavia must have been light years away and there was always the risk of him meeting a young Welsh girl who would sweep him off his feet. No doubt Henry had the same concerns about his girlfriend being attracted by another man. In the event, neither needed to worry; they both stayed loyal, and eventually married in 1922.

With no telephone or e-mail to use, the only contact was by the written word, and their regular letters were a joy to receive, and some 90 years later are a joy to read. They show the simple innocence in the way life was conducted at that time, and how even people educated at Chale School could demonstrate their love for each other from miles apart.

All the letters were faithfully kept, all in their original envelopes, probably read only once or twice. The following extracts are just a sample of their unique record of life during the Great War in a small village, with all the fears which went with life in a war. As elsewhere. the words, and spelling, are theirs.

1916

From Henry - 11th January - *Thank you for the letter, and the County Press. The weather has been bad, but I hope it is better tonight as we have to go on night work using barb wire, and that's bad enough without wind and rain.*

From Octavia - 24th May - *You had better send your socks down to me. I could manage to do that for you. The Sprake Maids* (the Sprake sisters - her sisters) *all send their love to you!*

From Octavia - 28th May - *The Postman told us he had seen several shoals of Mackerel, so I hope they will catch some.* (Her family had been Mackerel fishermen for at least 150 years).

Octavia Sprake centre back row

From Octavia - 16th June - *It's been rather an exciting time here today. This morning there was an Aeroplane came over, it was flying very low and it pitched in a ploughed field near Becksfield* (between Chale Green and Kingston, about half a mile from Octavia's home), *towards Kingston Farm. We all rushed over to see what had happened to it. There was only one man in it; he came from Gosport and was going to Bournemouth and took the wrong course, got lost in the clouds, the machine gave out, so he was obliged to descend. He had no idea he was on the Isle of Wight. When running the engine along to stop it, it turned over. He was not hurt, only a good bang on the nose.*

Then this afternoon another one came and pitched in that big field this side of Becksfield. He brought a man with him to overhaul the other aeroplane. This evening we have been watching them straighten it up, and the soldiers put ropes onto it and drawed it up through the field to the gate, so they were going to guard it tonight. There have been quite a crowd of people out there to look at it so it have been a bit lively!

From Octavia - 19th June - *They have been catching Mackerel most days; do you feel you would like one?*

From Henry - 24th October - *I hope the War will soon be over, but it does not seem very near at present as far as I can see, but still we must cheer up and always look on the bright side and trust that all will come right in the end. I should just like to go for a ride with you along the country road like ours.*

From Henry - 8th November - *I am very sorry to hear about Tom's mates being killed.* (Tom was Octavia's cousin, and Henry's friend, and he was in France at the time). *I hope please God that he will get home safe. It must be very hard to bear when it happens like that. I wonder when this war will end; I wish it was over now as I want to get back to you. We had some more men go to France last night, and some more today.*

From Henry - 18th November - *I had a nice letter from Uncle Jim in France. He tells me he has got the Military Medal. I wonder what I shall get if I ever go out; whether it will be medal, metal, or a cross* (a medal to wear; be hit by a bullet; or be killed), *but I don't worry and I trust in God to bring me back safe, and I believe he will.*

From Henry - 2nd December - *I shall not be able to come home for a week or two, so we will have to wait. Now you must cheer up and not be downhearted but you will have to give me an extra loving when I do come, so don't forget now will you.* (I don't think the meaning of these words is what it would be today!!).

From Henry - 9th December - *I had a letter in which they say there are some young ladies at Northgrounds and that they were wearing breeches; I should like to see them. We must go down round that way when I come home. Good-bye for the time being, with best love from your little Soldier boy, Henry.*

From Henry - 13th December - *Do you ever feel lonely and wish that I was there to be with you? I get that feeling sometimes but it's no use so I have to rub it in and get over it the best way I can. Have you seen anybody up home* (The Clarendon Hotel) *lately; go in just to check and ask them how I am getting on. I can see you doing that, I expect you will box my ears when I come for asking you to do that!*

From Henry - 24th December - *I hope to go to Church tomorrow morning at 7.00am. We have been very busy decorating our huts, putting up evergreens, paper chains, and I finished by helping to blacklead the stove and scrubbing the tables which we had just been standing on, so I have been enjoying myself. We will have Turkeys and Geese, with stuffing, then sauce and plum puddings and a pint of beer or minerals for each man.*

From Henry - Christmas Day 1916. *We have had a good Christmas Day; I can truly say I felt very happy. The hut looked smart. We had tables running down each side of the hut, and one across the top to carve on, and there were about a hundred seated in each hut. We had four carving in each hut and five or six more to serve. We had stuffed Turkey, and Geese; Brussell Spouts, and Potatoes, and then Plum Puddings and Sauce. We all enjoyed it very much.*

1917

From Henry - 1st February - …I can't wait any longer and you know 'delays are dangerous'. Remember what your father says, there is forgiveness for being too fast, but I think to take things on the whole I am a bit too slow! So you think you would have a difficult job to write down what you think about me; well I expect you would sometimes when I send one of those - what shall I call, Cheeky, or fast letters that I have no business to write, but as you know I feel a bit 'wicked' at times and I must let vent somehow.

From Henry - 24th March - I was talking to some chaps up here and one of them said he was from the Isle of Wight, and had worked out Billingham. I asked him if he knew where 'Corner' (Sprake's Brewery) was and he said "He bet he did" "He should like to be along side a good pint of old Sprack's now", so I for mischief says, "I would like to be beside one of his daughters". "Would you" he says, "which one, Octavia?". "Yes," I said, "that's the one, do you know her". "I should think I do", he said, so I began to think I had better stop quiet and change the subject, or I may be getting into trouble.

From Octavia - 26th March - Fancy you meeting another Isle of Wight Calf. I can't remember the man at all. There were so many working out there they used to come along in the evenings; it must be four or five years ago, and fancy him remembering my name, but there, I suppose it is such a striking one that he never forgot! Well, on Sunday after Church I walked along to the gate with your Mother, and then we went in; she was very jolly!

From Henry - 1st April - Another draft left here for France today. They keep thinning us out, but it's not my turn yet, but I suppose it is the fortunes of War and what is to be will be, as the saying goes.

From Henry - 8th April - I am glad you liked my letter and I think that I must have had, as you say, a good mood on just at the time. Sometimes however I have what I think you would term a rather naughty mood, you know when I feel kind of wicked like as if I would like to torment some young lady, or take one for a walk. You know how I mean without telling you.

From Octavia - 9th April - I had my first experience in driving the Motor by lamp light; I got on very well.

From Henry - 12th April - Fancy you staying up late to write love letters to a soldier, what ever would people say if they knew. I am glad you are getting on well with the driving by lamp light. I would very much like to be with you on a journey like that, but I am thinking we would want to stop on the road for we could not drive the motor and (talk and spoon) at the same time, or do you think we could manage both at once, eh!…. I think I will have 40 winks now, and dream of you.

From Henry - 17th April - *Busy darning pants, socks, etc. Two of us at it, one writing love letters and boiling water for supper, and me darning!*

From Octavia - 17th April - *We went for a walk down to Atherfield today. There have been some German mines washed up lately, so we went to see the one at Sheppards Chine. It was a long way farther down than the Coastguard Station. I had never been down that far before. We seen the thing, it was fastened to the cliff by a rope. It looked like a Copper turned up, but the explosive parts had been taken away. One of the Soldiers down at the Coastguard Station showed us a piece that came out of it.*

From Henry - 24th April - *I believe you were a bit lively Saturday night when you wrote that letter for although you did not put anything that way inclined in it I believe I can read between the lines!*

From Octavia - 8th May - *I am so thankful I have got such a good sweetheart.*

From Henry - 17th May - *I am sorry to hear that poor Arthur Harvey has been killed poor chap, but he did his duty. I think a dead hero is better than a live coward, although it's hard to die. Lets get the war over with, although I am afraid it will be a long time yet.*

From Henry - 23rd May - *Have you seen anything of Marjorie Cheek since she got married. I have heard that she has gone as thin as a rake. It seems as if married life does not agree with her if that is so!*

From Octavia - 28th May - *They are going to have a Treat at the Rectory tomorrow. Arthur Sprake is going off tomorrow to join up. I wonder what they will put him in? How terrible about the Air Raid on the South East Coast last Friday, so many killed and injured. We have been working on the land today. We have started planting potatoes over in the field, and hope to finish them tomorrow.*

From Henry - 10th June - *I have often thought of the ten minutes or so we sat on the seat 'down Heath' talking of things in general, and yet sitting there quite happy and contented. Oh Dear! I wish I could get home and have a quiet evening with you, only we will have to wait a long while yet. I hear there are more Chale chaps going off soon, but I expect they will enjoy it. How's Will's baby getting on. I suppose nobody else has any more knocking about, have they, and are there any more weddings coming off?*

From Octavia - 20th July - *I have not been out much with the Motor lately. I can only go off alone when it is a light load and we can rely on someone taking the tubs out for me. (Brewery deliveries).*

Henry wrote and told Octavia about the accident which removed parts of two of his fingers, when hit by a pile driver whilst erecting fence posts on a training exercise.

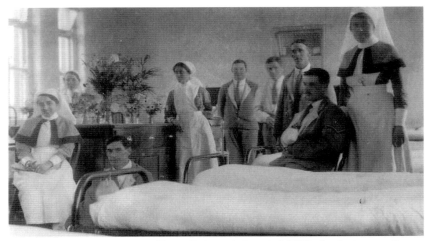
Henry Roberts in hospital 1917 after losing two fingers

From Octavia - 25th July - I would like to know if the hand, or any other of your fingers are injured. You said only the tops of two, but I wonder if any more are hurt. Please do not keep anything from me. We had a special service on Monday evening to dedicate the War Shrine which Mrs Gibbs of South View has given. It is fixed on the wall outside where we sit in Church facing Ridett's. Mrs Gibbs unfastened it. It is like folded doors, and the Roll of Honour is done out down the sides, and the names of those that are gone are in the centre. There were prayers, and then we sang a War Hymn, and then the names were read out, and we finished up with the National Anthem. (The shrine is now inside the Church on the west wall).

From Octavia - 26th July - The Chale and Shorwell Girls Friendly Society has done the Empires Honour down at Yafford House, like we did at Rectory last year. They have done it for Shorwell Church, and the District Nurses Fund this time. There were a lot of people there.

From Octavia - 30th July - There was a concert up Rectory last night on the lawn. It was a little wet but we kept dry under the big tree where you come in. The Scouts performed, and the Wolf Cubs did the Morris Dance. One of the Miss Pinnocks played the violin, and the other recited. Mrs Heald (the Rectors wife) gave a Recitation. They collected over £6.

From Octavia - 4th August - There is going to be a grand affair at Carisbrooke on Monday when Princess Beatrice is going to inspect the I.W. Boy Scouts, and the Marquis and Marchioness of Carisbrooke are going to be there, so all the Scouts and Wolf Cubs from here will be there. This is the third anniversary of the War. I hope, please God, we may soon have peace.

From Octavia - 30th August - A mine was washed in against the rocks at Rocken End and exploded last Saturday morning at about 5.00am. It shattered the doors and windows at South View. We heard the noise down here at Chale Green. It was a good job there was no one on the shore near there at the time, as there is a lot of timber and different stuff washed in.

Town Lane
Chale
I.W

Saturday evening

My dear Henry

I received your letter yesterday afternoon, it was not long in coming I should think you did have quite a lot of reading to do, with so many letters coming the same time. I am pleased to hear you are still getting on alright, and am still smiling, I went to the Concert, Thursday evening, it went off very well, and the room was packed I seen Riddle yesterday, & he told me they took £7. 10 I believe that was what he said. It made quite a change having different ones, taking part in it. I am sending you the Programme, for you to see what we had, as I didn't know if anyone would send you it. it is done out grand, don't you think; one of the Soldiers did them, he is very clever at sketching, he has done a lot of different things for the Cooke's Well now who let you know that I was at Church

and that I did not go in up home, it seems as if news does travel very quickly. It does seem so sad, these ships getting torpedoed, have you heard yet, if any of them were drowned from the Ivernia. We are having very cold weather, it has been snowing a bit this evening, I expect you find it, when you are on night work, how often as you get that in a week. Well cheer up we must all try & look on the bright side of things, and hope for better times. With love
Yours very truly
Octavia
P.S. I suppose you have heard G. Parker is home

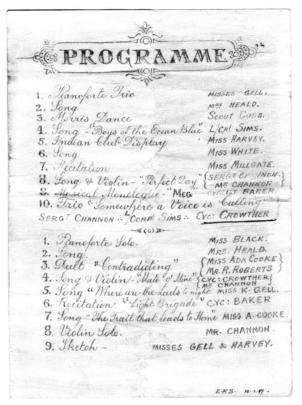

Programme of Concert in Chale January 1917 and letter from Octavia Sprake with news of the Concert

From Octavia - 10th October - *I enclose a programme of the Concert at the Scouts Hall. It was done by one of the Soldiers all grand; he is very clever at sketching. They raised £7.10/-.*

From Henry - 4th November - *How about the ship; is she still there or gone again? I hope they are able to get something out of her. It has been a lovely evening and I was thinking how nice it would be if we could only go for a good long walk again together. I have been soldiering two years and it doesn't seem very long, yet I have only been back from home two weeks and that seems a jolly long time.*

From Octavia - 8th December - *The Soldiers over Shorwell have been busy this week. The Motor Transports have been up and down past here all the day; they are clearing out over there altogether and are going to take the huts down, so they say. I suppose then it is right Mr Newnham is going to get married next Monday as he wrote and told you so. No, I am not going over to see it, for it would be too much like wasting time.* (Octavia probably did not 'approve' as he had been living with Miss Saunders before they got married - a waste of time getting married?).

From Henry - 28th December - *Thank you for the Christmas presents which will be very useful. You say it is very difficult to know what a soldier really wants; well one of the very best things he can have and should always try to keep, and what I am very pleased to say I have got, and will always stick to, is a God-fearing, true, and loving sweetheart. She may be miles away from him and he may not see her for months but she is one of the greatest blessings and help a man can really have especially when he really loves and respects her. How true those words are that "A woman can make a man an angel or a '....'" - you know what I mean. I do not know how long it will be before I am able to come and see you again, my darling, and trust that God will bring us home smiling, and I'll do the same.*

There were numerous letters sending news of old school friends having been killed or wounded, and regular comments such as *"I wish I could write such nice letters as you." "But they say 'The sweetest thoughts are the ones unspoken' - isn't that right?"*

It was not long before Henry Roberts was sent over to France, but as will be seen elsewhere, he returned safely, and married his beloved Octavia with whom he spent the rest of his life, in Chale.

Extracts from sundry other letters kept for over 85 years:-

To Henry from Mrs E Woodford of Denhams Cottage - 26th November 1916. *There has been some casks of paraffin oil and tubs of grapes and oranges washing in on the shore. The grapes were alright, not a bit salty, but the oranges were very bitter!*

To Henry from a friend when he was in hospital. - *We are sorry to hear of your misfortune, but thank goodness it's no worse, although it is bad enough, and you wont be able to handle the rifle so it will save you the trouble to go and kill Germans, or being killed by them! There were two young fellows by us killed last week, and only 20 years of age.*

From Charlie Parker in France - 18th August 1917. *I'm sorry to hear about your fingers, but I think it's more good luck than bad as it is likely to keep you in Blighty because it's no cop out here. We are not near the line now, but I am sorry.*

From C.J. Creeth - 28th July 1917. *A Regimental Board of Enquiry was held on your accident one day this week but I have not gleaned any details yet. I see in todays paper that Jack Seely is going to be married again to a widow, Mrs Nicholson. He has been staying at Brook House recovering from the accident that happened in France. Do you know Amy Downer at Shorwell; she teaches the Infants in the school and plays the organ in the church. She was engaged to Jim Cox, a sailor man who went down with Kitchener. Well, she was married a few days ago to a soldier chap, a widower. A very smart girl. I am told that a War Shrine has been given to Chale Church by Mrs Gibbs; there was a service held recently to consecrate it.*

Diet sheet for training camp - October 1916:-

Breakfast 7.00am	- Tea, bread and butter, bacon and tomatoes.
Light meal	- Bread, cold beef, pickles, tea.
Haversack ration	- Bread, cheese or meat.
Dinner 5.00pm	- varied - Roast and cabbage, potatoes.
	Stewed apples and custard.
	- Irish stew & dumplings, potatoes.
	Fig roll.
	- Roast Beef, potatoes, peas.
	Stewed prunes.
	- Roast and cauliflower, potatoes.
	Stewed peaches and custard.

On his demobilization Henry Roberts received £29.4.3d., and the Meritorious Service Medal. He was certified free from vermin and scabies; his boots and clothing were returned in a clean and serviceable condition; and he returned three blankets. On his discharge he received a Certificate showing he had qualifications as a Carpenter, and 'as a help to find civil employment' it was stated that he was employed on Defences while in the 3rd Army. He was in charge of working parties, and proved himself most capable in supervising labour. He was also employed at his trade as a carpenter and has done office work and has proved himself an all round excellent N.C.O.

Well done Henry!

Uncle Jim

Throughout his service in the Army, Henry never forgot his Uncle Jim, James Senior, his mother's brother. Letters home frequently asked for news of his uncle.

James Senior lived with his sister in Chale Rectory when he left school, and probably started working in The Clarendon Hotel as a 'boots'. He married and went to live in London, and worked as a waiter in hotels. When the Great War broke out in 1914, James joined the army as a rifleman in the King's Royal Rifle Corps. and soon found himself serving in the trenches in France. Uncle Jim was a great family man and often wrote to his relatives in Blighty, writing from within the trenches. In a letter in 1916 he sent some pressed Pansies for another sister's birthday. He commented that he had picked the pansies off the top of the trenches, *"…but he could not get more as there were too many shells flying about while he was writing…"*. He was in 'the Verdun affair'.

In 1917 he wrote to Henry. (The letters were all censored). *"We are having a decent dose of it up here this time. We have lost all count of it and don't know when we finish as yet. I have had one near touch since we have been up here. I was rolled over by a Wiz Bang, and got cordite and shrapnel dust in my face and just broke the skin on my shoulder. I had to be innoculated in the chest for it but felt alright so that was lucky and I did not think it worth mentioning in any of my letters to the others. We have been in some very warm corners but got out alright and I hope we keep at it.*

"We see a few of your fellows (Henry's men were Engineers, and not riflemen!), *they seem a decent lot. I was with one of them when I was rolled over; we call them the gentlemen of the crowd!"*

By October 1917, when Henry was recovering in hospital from his accident, Jim found himself in a Liverpool hospital, wounded for the third time, and wrote to him. *"I am waiting to be marked out soon. I expect it will be convalescence but don't know which way they send you from here. I got a beauty through the left buttock and groin and shrapnel in both knees. It is almost healed up already. It was about the luckiest shot of the day. The bullet never touched a nerve or anything, and it worked out as I was walking back to the Dressing Station, so I've had no trouble with it. I could have carried on quite well if I liked, but I was fed up before we started over so I told them I was out for a Blighty so I turned back as soon as I was hit.*

"This is the third time he has hit me and not done any damage so he will have to try again. It is alright going over the top now. We go over with our rifles slung and smoking, it is just like a moving wall. You can only see a few yards round and hear rifles cracking as the guns are one continual roar". No doubt this was to reassure young Henry that being in the trenches was really quite fun.

At the same time, Jim Senior wrote to his sister Grace Roberts reassuring her not to worry about Henry being in hospital with his injured fingers - "..*they will keep him in as long as possible. I hope he will not have to go over the water; one of us is enough and I am used to it that I don't notice it, although if he got over he would not get in the line very much, but there are many worse places than that!*

"*They seem to be having a pretty warm time with the raids in London. I think they return it with interest by the machines that go over his way every day. He used to come and visit us every night when we were under canvas waiting to join the battalion. Don't send me another parcel yet as it may go astray and I don't feel like them getting the benefit of it. "I do not think the War will last such a long time as they have given us a rise in wages, when we get it. We never know when we are going to draw any. They take away your pay book as soon as you come over and you never know how you stand, but you don't want very much the other side anyhow. Tobacco is the best, a smoke is a fine thing for the nerves. We all went over the top smoking. I nearly dropped my pipe when I was hit. It is just as though you were walking behind a wall that was moving as you can only see a few yards ahead, and all you hear is rifle fire as the big guns are one long roll. It is really a fine sight. I should not have come away when I was hit, only I was fed up as they had moved me to another part just before we went over.*"

Little was heard of Jim Senior after that. He returned to France once again, but on 21st March 1918 he was taken Prisoner of War. When Henry Roberts returned home in 1919, he was determined to find out where his uncle was. Reports in the papers indicated that there were still three unidentified soldiers suffering from shell shock, and Henry wrote to the War Office to see if one of these might possibly be his Uncle Jim. He received a reply to say that the official report was that Rifleman J. Senior had been reported by the German Authorities as having died as a P.O.W. on 19th May 1918 from 'feverish intestinal catarrh and heart failure'.

Shortly after, a letter was received by Jim's widow, from a Sergeant Armstrong - "*Yes, I knew your husband very well indeed. Although I was only attached to the 8th, I got to know him very well. He and I were fortunate to be captured March 21st 1918. We agreed to stand by each other while prisoners.*

But whilst at Flavey le Nartel, hard work, filth, no sleep, and starvation killed dozens of men. The Germans stated 'Bronchitis, Tuberculosis, Heart Disease', in fact anything but what was right.

I was with your husband when he died, he would have liked to have told me something but he was far too weak, I let him understand by showing him your address that I would acquaint you. He was never at Stendal Camp. This is an account of his movements.

Captured 21st March. Marched to Rebermont through the night. Kept in a garden for three days without food. Stayed there until April 1st when we moved to Megiere where we stayed about ten days in a Church. April 10th we moved by road to Flavey le Nartel; the hard work there, little sleep, no food, almost killed everyone. I know your husband was not a weak man, but he got so thin and weak that he could not move, and a dirty, verminous, damp clay floor was his bed. After a while he was put into a hut where there were beds of straw, but he died on 19th May. I believe that anxiety had a lot to do with his rapid failing for he talked of his home several times. I left his papers with the British Red Cross because I thought it was only a matter of time with myself. The cruelty of the Germans was such as I shall never erase from my mind.

The pleasure is mine, and would have been great if only I could have given you good news.

Yours. A. Armstrong."

Uncle Jim had served his King and Country for some four years, and died aged 43, still a Private Soldier. He had been wounded three times; had been awarded the Military Medal (M.M.), and the Distinguished Conduct Medal (D.C.M.); and died in the 'care' of the enemy as a P.O.W. As Henry had remarked, 'A Dead Hero is better than a live coward'. Perhaps his accidental loss of two fingers had saved him from a similar end.

Any further letter on this subject should be addressed to—

The Secretary, War Office,
Finsbury Court,
Finsbury Pavement,
London, E.C.2,
and the number below quoted.

Telephone : LONDON WALL 4720.

C.2.Casualties.861425.

WAR OFFICE,

FINSBURY COURT,

FINSBURY PAVEMENT,

LONDON, E.C.2.

26 January 1920.

Sir,

In reply to your letter of 28th December concerning 4528 Rifleman J.Senior, 8th Battalion, King's Royal Rifle Corps, I am directed to inform you with regret that it has been officially reported by the German Authorities that he died as a Prisoner of War on 19th May 1918 from feverish intestinal catarrh and heart failure. This report has been officially accepted and there cannot unfortunately be any reason to doubt its accuracy.

In the circumstances it is impossible that he might be amongst those soldiers, now only two in number, who are unidentified in consequence of mental trouble. If however, it will assist you to reconcile your mind to the fact of his death, any photograph of your Uncle you will forward to this office will be compared with those of these two men and the result communicated to you.

I am to return herewith the stamped addressed envelope you forwarded, and to add that the case of Private Howe is being dealt with separately.

I am,
Sir,
Your obedient Servant,

Mr. T.H.Roberts,
Clarendon Hotel,
Chale,
Isle-of-Wight.

"Uncle Jim" official notification of his death, twenty months after

CHAPTER 6

BUTTER, APPLES, AND A DRUNKEN COOK!

Whilst Henry Roberts was training in the Royal Engineers in Wales he kept every letter he received, and the following extracts are taken from a selection from his mother, Grace Roberts, of The Clarendon Hotel. The concern for her son, and the need to keep him supplied with butter was a regular part of her letters, but they give an idea of what life was like in Chale during the second half of the Great War.

Pte Henry Roberts

1915

Nov 13th - *I miss you a lot. Do you need a scarf. Have you got your Kharki yet?*

Nov. 17th - *Charlie Parker came home Saturday and he was married in the morning and has gone back today.*

Nov. 22nd - *I am sending your pants and only one pair of socks. I expect they will not be quite big enough in the feet if you have a lot of marching. You did not say about your washing. Will they wash for you and air it, if not post it home and I will have it done for you and mended. I am having to feed the 20 soldiers we have here; I did not want to do it but they wanted me to feed them so I have an orderly who comes in every day to wash up and do the potatoes. They have some old plates and cups, all the enamel chipped off. One of the men here says you must be careful how you put your putties on, not too tight or they make your veins swell up! I am sending some potted beef with your pants and socks, but don't keep it about too long as I made it the other day. I thought you could have it at night, and the butter with your Coffee and morning tea. Mind you let me know if you want any more shirts.*

December 1st - *Did you get the parcel with your pants in? Don't forget when you have time to get your photo done. You have not told me who is doing your washing?*

December 3rd - *I am sending a parcel with some more butter to fill you up.*

December 7th - *I tell the soldiers we will have to call it Clarendon Barracks now. We have all the Bugle Calls, they have just called for tea; the next call will be 9.30. They miss early morning and lights out! The men get 8/6 a week. We have 4 sergeants and they get in the lunch room and gamble all Sunday afternoon, and some chaps have not a penny left, it is dreadful.*

December 20th - *I will send you some butter tomorrow but don't keep it too long as it may go a little strong as they have given the cows Mangol.*

1916

January 2nd - *Dad has bought a horse for £20 and a Landau for £12.10/-, and a whip at the sale in Cowes.*

January 17th - *There are 28 soldiers come down Terrace, men and boys. The officers are staying here. I am sending you 4 hard boiled eggs; I thought you might eat them at night. Don't keep them too long, they were done this morning. Will Brown said of the ship he came home in, the bottom was loaded with cattle; the middle with ammunition; and the top with men!*

January 19th - *Dad shot 16 pidgeons; we had them for the men for dinner yesterday with Beef. They were very good, stewed all night in the oven. They tell me coal is £2.10/- now. (Presumably a ton).*

January 28th - *Hope you are getting on all right. I enclose some snowdrops from the rockery. We have had some more calves so we will have more milk now and I can send you some butter.*

February 1st - *Dad has sold the Landau and another at Niton. Lots of Soldiers about 50 in Chale, staying here awaiting the new huts to be ready and before going off for training. We have the men in doing up the rooms, they make a lot of mess, I shall be glad when they are done.*

February 3rd - *We had a ship on Brook ledge this morning, 11 men on board. They could not get near with the lifeboats, the men had to jump over, and 9 was brought in safe, and one dead. The Captain would not leave the ship, they say now he is drowned. I belive the ship has gone down; I cannot see it from the windows.*

February 10th - *We had the Beagles meet here today. They had a good run and put up two hares. I don't know if they killed one.*

February, 15th - *Dr Armstrong says Riddle (Ridley, Henry's brother) will be all right when he has his teeth out. All the men were examined by him yesterday, some for General, some for F.... (France?) some for*

Home Service. One was cissy as a crooked mile, they passed him for F.... . Its been dreadful windy in Chale; last night it blew the sky light off and broke the glass and hinges.

February 16th - I was surprised to hear you had got a stripe so soon, We all wish you the best of luck and hope you keep it and get another soon. Don't mention it when you write as some round here will be jealous. When Mrs Brown took Hector (her son) to have a tooth out, he sat down and the dentist closed all the windows before he bagan. Poor Hector screamed and kicked. She worked her arm up and down and kept saying 'Stick to it boy, stick to it'. I don't know if it was the tooth or the chair, however he left them both behind! You must stick to it, not leave it behind!

April 9th - I had a Vacuum Cleaner out from Mr Sharpes, goes back in the morning. It was pretty fun doing the carpets, it brings out the dust. I got a Cook come in last evening, Mrs Cole I hope she will get on alright if only she does not drink too much. She can chatter, her tongue does not get rusty for lack of use! We have just heard young Courtney Woodford was killed in the trenches by a sniper. So sad for his Mother and Father (they lived in part of Denhams).

May 24th - Mrs Cropper sent £1 for me to send her 2lb butter every week she likes it so much.

May 30th - Frank Cheek (the hotel 'boots') had the sack Friday. He took the new horse out when Dad was away; he was drunk, fell off. He was not hurt; lucky it was by Brown's (the shop) and the horse went in the stable yard and never got away. They have caught some Mackerel yesterday.

June 1st - I am sending you a little Mackerel, Ridley was down on shore and caught about 20; don't keep it too long. Dad sold a calf the other day for £8.15/-; never had such a price before. You will see in the County Press that Arthur Sprake is alright as long as he does the Carrying.

June 6th - Just a line to tell you poor Albert Rayner has been very badly burned at the Battle of Jutland, and there is a Wire up at Browns saying Lord Kitchener and others gone down last night. What ever are we coming to?

June 15th - They buried poor Albert on Tuesday morning at 11.00am. A nice funeral; the soldiers fired over him, and the choir went. Nasty accident down Chapel Corner at lunchtime, a young Officer on his motor bike went bang into Bartletts Charabang, they think his head and leg was hurt.

June 19th - Dad bought some pigs at Niton and he lost one out of the van, but he caught it. Then when he got home at 10 o'clock, the same one got out again and they lost it for about 1½ hours. Went all over Chale looking for it. I was nearly asleep when it walked into the kitchen. I told Mrs Cole after they all went to bed that it was all the Fun of the Fair!

July 5th - *We have got some Soldiers in, instead of 14 they sent 18. I could not take them all, so some are sleeping out at other houses but coming here for their meals. We are very busy.*

July 11th - *The poor Count came in this morning. I think he threw his paper down and Mrs Cole flew at him, they said like mad. She told him he was the fellow who sat all day in the chair and she could not move it, and she was swearing. Ted Sheppard said they nearly had a row, she was a real bully. I don't think anybody likes her. Mr Way jammed his finger in his safe yesterday morning, took the end off on his left hand. They say they have taken poor old Ruben Edmonds away last week for he was hammering his head with a hammer. I am not sure if he has gone to the Work House, or the Lunatic Asylum.* (Ruben died soon afterwards in the Lunatic Asylum, and was buried at Chale).

July 13th - *I shall have to have another girl. I went and saw one yesterday in Newport. We had tea in Harvey's and I think she quite enjoyed it. We had the carriage open and drove through Rookley; the hedges are lovely there, better than through Chillerton.*

August 4th - *It is a real rush with so many visitors coming and going. Mrs Cole has been drunk every day since last Saturday and I have had to do most cooking every day. The new girl came in the pantry when I was washing up. I asked her what was the matter and she said Mrs Cole never let her alone this morning. Dad got up early and went out before Mrs Cole was down and walked in the Cellar when she was helping herself to beer. She was very ill and said she had been sick all night. I just told her that if she had not so much beer she would be better. I told her every day she had too much, she looked and said she did not think so, however she has done much better, but when pay day came on Sunday she was off! I sent you only 1lb butter as we were all pushed up.* (Not enough butter to meet orders).

August 8th - *I sent off the new girl this morning, she was home sick, gave me the hump. I suppose you don't know a nice Welsh girl worth having?*

August 22nd - *We are very busy. We had a tennis party yesterday, and Ridley had 20 on the lawn for tea. Lots of coming and going. I get on with Mrs Cole a little better since I gave her a good dressing down, but she is slack. I got a girl from school; she does very well but she is only 13, anyway we jog on! Next day - I hear the soldiers coming in for tea, but Winnie can do that, she does well for one so young. Charlie Dabell came to see Dad about milk rising to 5d a quart from 1st September. I said, what about cream. He said has always been 2/6 a quart so must be 2/6d. I told them its no use raising one without the other. Dad has gone to Yaverland and Brading today with Miss Rawson.*

August 25th - *We had a bit of fun the other night. A lady called me to look at a light on the Veranda. I* told her it was Portland. *Well, bye and bye I saw a light on the bottom of the lawn, matches striking, and someone creeping. Dad was out so I went down. All the visitors but two ladies, one a Captain's wife, had gone to bed. Well, it was so dark they could not see me walking along, so when they got to the pantry window, Peter (the dog) was with them. I heard one say there is someone on the other side. So I said 'Who's there', it was the Sergeant. They had seen the light in the top room and come to see what it was. When I spoke they was a bit scared, and he said 'Is that you, Ma' I said 'Yes'. They nearly fell in the big ditch, and they were all scratched.* (it does not say, but I presume she meant that it was the Captain's wife and the Sergeant) *Well, what about that!!*

September 8th - *Browns* (at the shop) *are giving up the post office as Tawny* (Trelawny, their son) *is going away* (in the Army) *Ridley is going to write and see if he can get it and have it here in the Hotel if the Royal Brewery will let us do this. I think Browns are upset about Tawny and they are giving it up in the hope they will be asked to keep it on. Don't say a word but Dad heard that Browns do not get on with Head one, a Mr Cox, and they will not ask them to keep it if possible. We had a doctor staying here this week. Dad took him to Brooke and he noticed he was limping, so he looked at his knee. He said it was 'screws' and was caused by bad teeth and he should have them seen to at once. Dad was surprised, and we all had a good laugh!*

September 15th - *Have heard that Mrs Harris has got the Post Office. Ridley tried for it, but it would have been a great tie for him. We heard on Monday that the butcher from Mr Newnham's with one eye had to go* (to join up) *he thought he was safe, and Arthur Sprake has got off for another two months. They say Mr Cook, Mr Woodford, Mr B.Chiverton, and Mr J.Brown is the head of all this stir up about here. We hear Major Dean has been over the road for young Linington. He kept coming up Chale every night on his bike to play tennis with Nora Harvey just before she married. Over the way is getting the name up again for being busy bodies.*

September 25th - *We have two young ladies in; they say their father* (Sir Sam Fay) *has bought North Grounds. There has been an Air Raid over Portsmouth last night. Mr Thompson and his sister watched it for two hours; it was lovely.*

October 23rd - *We heard last night that the poor old Count is killed in France.*

December 22nd - *We will be quiet for Christmas, only about 14. Dad has got to take people to Newport in the morning and back at night. We have sent two Guinea Fowls and two ducks to Mr Thompson. Have a happy Christmas and go to Church.*

1917

January 1st - *Happy New Year. What do you think, young Harvey has had your white ferret. It went into his garden and he put it in the Wash House to find rats; it found some then went to sleep after he gave it bread and milk. I said it was a good thing it did not get my pullets. Mr Cook says there will be nearly 70 coming to the feast on Saturday. We had Sir Sam Fay in, he is down to look at his farm. They say he is going to buy John Brown's cottages.*

January 4th - *Uncle Ted went out on Tuesday night to find some eggs, the board in the fowl house gave way and he fell down and sprained his leg; if he had not had the case (plaster) on he would have broken his thigh again.*

January 8th - *We had our Supper Party at the Scouts Hall on Saturday night. It all went off very well indeed without any fuss. It was much better being cold, but we had hot potatoes and Xmas pudding, I think they all had two helpings! We had cold roast beef, tongue, ham, boiled beef, and a half leg of mutton. There were school children and Scouts, and young Scouts or Cubs as they call them. Over 60 sat down including Fathers and Mothers*

Sir Sam Fay - a regular guest at The Clarendon Hotel

January 15th - *I enclose a photo of Sir Sam Fay from the Daily Mail; thats the man who has bought Northgrounds, its very like him! Also a programme for the concert at the Scouts Hall; its was full and some had to stand up. When Mr Starks was in the Bar we was having a crack about sugar, so this fellow who was having dinner he says, "Why is sugar so scarce"; "We can get plenty" so says I.*

January 22nd - *The weather is very cold. The poor chaps (soldiers) here have just a tiny stove down Cliff Terrace. Mrs Cropper finds them one gallon of oil to burn for a week, very good of her. The chap at Ladder says they are alright but it is dreadful for them. I have never seen Chale in such a state as now. From our front door right over the road is ice. There is no wind so the cold is not so bad. I have not been out, you can hardly stand. Dad went down Rectory to tell them not to go to Shanklin today; he turned round near Granny's and down he went, got nothing worse than a good shake up. Crowther came back on leave last week. He had to walk from Ventnor, there was nothing at the Station. It was dreadful dark and he did not know the road; some wounded soldier told him what he could. It was so dark he had to strike matches to find his way. It took him 2 ½ hours.*

March 12th - *We have had two cow calfs born so we will have plenty of butter now. I will send you some more, and perhaps send some to Jim in France.*

March 15th - *We have a Soldier here who is a Jew; well he came this morning to learn me how to make Macaronie, so it was just all right. The worst part is you cannot make only to keep about one day. Another thing happened yesterday, Eva was out and a Carriage and Pair came to the front door with 4 people to tea, fancy, it nearly took my breath away. I told Frank to make the Macaronie. I heard the other day that Old Count who was here last Winter is not dead, someone has seen him in Bournemouth!*

March 19th - *We had a letter from a boy who was here with the Old Count. Well he went to France, came back with trench feet, they sent him to Epsom. When he got out at the Station he saw Old Count himself, there he was. Surprised never so much in his life, he thought him dead, so did we!*

April 2nd - *What a do about the beer trade, everybody wants to know what the other is going to do. We have not put ours up today, but we shall have to when this is gone. I don't know what The Clarendon will come to what with horse feed etc., well we must do the best we can. We have three vans going to Newport with the Scouts party and some school children going to see the pictures. We heard this morning that a German mine is washed in down on the beach at Atherfield. They have tied it on the Cliff and the Soldiers have to guard it so no one goes near it. I hope it does not go off and blow up the cliff. We had a Canadian gent in from the War Office looking for fossils at Atherfield, and he hopes to come again in a month, from London.*

April 6th - Good Friday morning - *We have had a lot of snow. It's 3ft deep in the hedges, and all down King Hall in the ditch ever so deep.*

April 11th - *There is another mine washed in yesterday. The papers say what a battle they have had, it is dreadful this week, and the loss of life.*

April 20th - *Did I tell you Mrs Cole wrote and told me she is leaving, but now she wants to come back, but I shall be myself this summer.*

April 23rd - *Poor Uncle Harry came yesterday, he looks very ill, so thin. Cicsy says he has had a lot to eat, but their lot is not much at the best! Cis says young Hanns is in France and about a month ago the Officer told him he was wanted by someone about 4 miles away, he could have the afternoon off. He went to see who it was and was shown into a very swell mess and a young man came to see him and asked if he knew him, it was young Seely, the poor chap that was killed just after. He said 'You rode with my cousins and your Sister in Law.' He asked if he had good boots and that he would save him 2 pairs of good French boots. You will see from the County Press that Miss Webb's maid fell over the cliff.*

May 4th - Mrs Chandler was helping me to wash yesterday, she said there was talk again that Lord Kitchener was not dead; I wonder if we will hear more about him. I had a letter from Mrs Cropper yesterday; she only wants me to pot her 2 jars of butter, 25lb each. Not me, I'm just going to write and tell her!

June 9th - We had about 49lbs butter this week, I'm going to pot some. I have 36lb ordered for potting at 1/8d. lb so that is not so bad. I did 34lb this week at 1/5d. per lb; fancy, in June 1916 the price was only 10d.lb. We have to make up for something, we don't sell much beer now at 6d a pint.

June 27th - We are very busy with the haymaking. I am just getting their tea ready for the field. We have so many in, if our house was twice the size we could let it. Tawny Brown wishes he was home and Arthur Sprake says he does not like it.

July 6th - Aunt Patience says she has plenty of rats for you to kill.

July 18th - We have lots of blackcurrants on Granny's trees and I have made some Jam with black sugar, we cannot get any sugar so I hope it will set. There is a lot of fruit about this year.

August 13th - We have so many in at the moment; we are so busy and have a full house.

August 16th - (A letter received from a relative in Leeds describes the horror of the War). 400 men are missing from Jim's Regiment. A train brought into Leeds on Friday night with 80 very bad stretcher cases and 168 sitting-up cases, everyone gassed, or this liquid fire that burns their eyes out poor things; it is terrible. Dad has just come back from Newport and said he saw Frances Russell's father who said his son is killed in France, and Jim Wheeler is also killed.

August 24th - Its been a rough night and all the shore is full of timber. Dad has gone down to Rocken End. We also had a dreadful lot of apples down, you should see the size of them. If you can cook them I will send you some. We are full up still. Mr Fardell the Court Clerk from Newport and his wife are here for a week. Olive Chandler put her arm through the lobby door window and had 2 stitches in it; her Mother comes in to help, but it makes it worse for me. We are so busy. We had over 40 for lunch and teas; I can tell you there is not much time to think. Dad has just come in, nothing worth much down shore.

Sept. 4th - Allen Cox is killed, poor man. Mrs Way sent me four green figs, and four peaches. I wanted to send you some but they were not good enough. There is another mine washing in down shore, and blew out some windows at Southview. Well, the day before Dad was just where it came in, and there was another empty one. There has been a lot of timber on the shore, and petrol, and some oil; Dad has been busy down Ladder getting it up.

Sept. 12th - *We are ever so busy still. We had 36 in for midday dinner. We have a bit of boiled beef, 18 ½ lbs. We had a mother and her daughter in, both widows. They were coming from Africa and their boat was torpedoed off Queenstown. The husband was drowned and she was in the water five hours in the night, poor thing. I do think some of the Irish are as bad as the Germans, vile beasts.*

Sept. 28th - *I heard today that carpenters are earning 8d an hour, that works out at £2 a week (60 hours a week) so you ought to be getting £1 a week at least. We have got a quiet house now; I expect Sir Sam Fay to make up 3 tonight. We have got some fresh men in. One old fellow did nothing but grumble the first night, he had been all over the World and never seen such a place as this. I told him to cheer up, he would soon be young again here. Well, he said today he was just getting used to it. He says he gets too much beer sometimes; then he don't get much for a time - he was moderate yesterday, he only had 10 pints. I said, well just think we don't get much now so keep quiet while you are here. He is an Old Soldier, they say there is no rest at night when he gets too many pints. Another old fellow that was a Sailor told me he offered him a rifle and five rounds and told him to go up into that field; after that he was quiet!*

October 25th - *Glad you got back alright. Dad sold two calves, one for £15 and the little one for £12.10/. He sold the old chestnut (horse) that was turned out in the field to O & R Sprake (brewery), I hope it goes on alright. I had my three top teeth out, and more on Tuesday; Rosa Sprake had three out. Just got 4 in for tea.*

October 31st - *I have to post 12lb of butter.*

November 5th - (Monday, Bonfire Night) - *We had a ship come in Friday just under South View Garden, they can look down on her there. She has coal on board, I wish we could get some here. Dad was down there Saturday and again today, I don't know what they are doing, there is no chance to unload her so far. I forgot to send you the leg of the hare you caught until too late. I was afraid it would not be good, so I ate it, and sent Nora Cook some of the gravy. She enjoyed it very much. She was very poorly yesterday and Saturday but now she is better. Mr Newnham and Mrs Saunders are going to get married, I hope they will be very happy. They have been 'boy & girl' together they say, so they must know each other.*

November 7th - *What a farce, we have to go to the Post Office to collect our letters now, at 5.00 o'clock. No time to write for the post then. We had a German mine washed ashore quarter mile near Wheelers and one near Ladder yesterday. They came and took parts out and this morning they brought gun Cotton and blew up the other. We had a good rattle with doors and windows. Ernie Wheeler had a ceiling blown down and some bricks off the chimney. No 1 and No 4 had some windows broke, but I am not sure about this! The coal ship is still there, can't do much about it, in fact nothing!*

November 17th - *The ship got off on Thursday. Dad got a little coal, over ½ ton, it burns well but not much heat from it but it does not burn away so quick in the rooms. Dad has been busy with the Carriage and weddings lately.*

November 24th - *Dad says they have no butter in Ryde; I can get 2/6 lb for butter by post.*

December 11th - *Mr Newnham's wedding went very well. Dad had the new carriage he bought. They had the breakfast at Sandrock, and then they had tea. What a dreadful time it is, there is plenty going on in France, poor things. Poor Wallie Barton is killed, and so many more.*

December 12th - (letter from Riddle) - *What shall we get for Mother for Christmas. A nice brush and comb would be nice as her old one is wearing out. Don't get one that will be difficult to clean; a nice plain one with a spray of leaves on it. What do you think?*

Shortly after this Henry was sent to France, and no further letters were found. What a wonderful character Grace Roberts must have been; what a glorious sense of humour. If only I had been able to meet her.

From THR (Thomas Henry Roberts)
to AOS (Ada Octavia Sprake) 18/1/19

CHAPTER 7

SHEEPS EYES, SWAN SOUP, AND DONKEY STEW

When young Henry Roberts of the Clarendon Hotel, Chale, left school he went to work for Dick Cox the local builder as an Apprentice, but later he worked as an assistant and slaughterman for Mr J. Newnham, Family Butcher of Niton Undercliffe. In November 1915 he was called up for Army Service. They were great friends, and Mr Newnham wrote frequent letters to young Henry. The following are extracts from these epistles. The spellings are his!

Mr J. Newnham

I would like the reader to contemplate the growing depression as the War progressed, and more and more young men died for their Country. This comes out in these letters; Mr Newnham is full of confidence at the start, but he gets more depressed about the situation as time goes on.

1915

Nov 15th - *I miss you very much but feel under the circumstances you are in the right place. I feel proud to think you are on the road <u>to Berlin</u>, for that is our goal. Plenty of food and work will make a man of you. You must grow a <u>maustache</u>* (he did) *and be a soldier proper. The Girls still come sighing around and look very sorrowful. Its Henry they want. I hope they will come with their orders, but you I think was the attraction! How they sigh. And when you come back I will say, Just come and see what I got, and they will be all right again. You must get on and be a rall of some kind. The old woman said her son was a rall, but it turned out he was a scaundrall. Suppose you get a V.C., what Ho, then for them Maids about here!*

Dec 3rd - *Thanks for your letter. I guess you look like a soldier now with your maustache waxed out to a point. And soldiers clothes, how smart you must look. I tell the young ladies, Henry sends his love to them, and it quite makes their eyes sparkle. Remember me to Lloyd George if you see him, and tell him he's not so bad after all. I hope they will get you ready for Berlin. You have a chance now to gain medals and crosses. Tom misses you in the slaughterhouse, trimming up, etc. We had a twister of an Ox this week 49-10, a real good one. Tom cut up the hind quarters this week, and cut the chucks off the fores., but he has no notion how to carry a big one, he does a small one all right.*

Dec 16th - *I was very pleased to get your Photo's. Tom was just about pleased and thought you look Capital, so do I. I miss you, and Tom misses you in the slaughterhouse. I wish you could be back for Christmas. We are very busy. We had 2 good steers from Chale Farm on Monday and one from Pyle next Monday, and a* <u>Show</u> *one for Christmas. Harry can't do much in the slaughter-house, or in carving the stuff. He dropped a full quarter on the shop floor, but he does his best. Yes, the 49 score Ox looked lovely. I should like the 2 little wethers; I guess they are full of fat inside.*

Dec 30th - *Thank you for the photos. I got the big one framed in the shop. I show them to the girls. It makes their* <u>Mouths Water</u>*! May Cotton wants the full length one; it was shabby of you not to send her one. I twisted up a bit of your love for her in a bit of paper but she would not have it unless you sent it. We had a good Xmas. We had a twister Ox, only 56.4, my God. He wanted some fingering. We had 2 prize sheep 15.8 so we had some good Mutton. Percy is going to retire on his Christmas Boxes; made a fortune! Peter (his young son) proper worships your Photo. He says thats Henry. Mr Reade lives like a fighting cock now, and looks as pert as a Chafer. Rump steaks and chops. Yes, Ruby's married; her little tricks must end now, for I reckon she has a master now! Cheer up and keep well because I want you to march into Berlin.*

1916

Jan 20th - *Thank you for your letter. I told Mrs Wright that May was in the Porch. She laughed at that. I can see just how sweet she was. Poor May, you should have given her a bit of a scrubbing, that would have pleased her. I pity her because her mouth waters for you. That little Shepherd girl, with the Sheep's eyes is in a deuce of a way about you. I had a message from her for you but I have forgotten it. It was kind of sweet like and I could see she meant it very much. So you must smack your lips over it and fancy you had* <u>something nice</u>*. When they come I tell them something that makes their mouths water, and that seems to please and satisfy them.*

Feb 7th - *I wish you were here to assist me. I miss you so much. No one to drive in a nail and keep it tidy. It makes one swear to see things let go to rack and ruin for want of a nail. I don't like this War any more. All that trenching you do, and on to barb wire. I guess the chaps did* <u>CUSS.</u> *God help any poor chap that gets hung up in it in action. Making one in the dark was worse than tieing sheep turds in a with. (A 'with' is an Isle of Wight word for a twisted wand of willow or hazel, used to bind faggots). I have not seen May. I guess she has made a Nun of herself. Poor May, needs comforting. She better have a Beauchamp (I think he means - Beechams). That I believe cures all ailments so they say. Miss Sheppard's eyes real glisten when I give her a message from you. It does much more good than a Beauchamp would. It is a real livener for her. It gives her a sweet feeling I can see! I'm glad you swank about a little. You might even claim a sort of relation to Lord Roberts. Why not? Anything to make up a tale.*

Feb 21st - *Congratulations on your promotion. A ral, truly man and thank God your not a scoundrel; quite right to obey orders. Well done Henry. What I would like to see you drill the defaulters on the Promenaude. Eyes right, chest out, etc. what is it you say. Tom is leaving on Tuesday. He has got unbearable for work, so slack, so dirty, so neglectfull that I had to keep on complaining. Then he heard me telling John White how slack he was, and nothing ever cleaned, and never up in the morning. He listened at the door, so his wife said, and heard what I said. But I was glad he did hear. She pitched into me like a pick pocket and brought back the meat I had given them for Sunday dinner, she did not want it. A while ago he was most insolent to me, so this morning when I paid him he said "I shall leave on Saturday", so I said "Very well", and that settled it. I let him go, he will miss me more than I will miss him. He would not get up in the morning, and the folk grumbling because they could not get the meat in time for dinner. Oh it will make the young ladies smile when I tell them Lance Corporal Roberts send his love to them. It will be worth a Jew's eye to them. I guess you are just beginning to* <u>swank</u> *now, strutting about proud as a hen with one chick.*

March 5th - *Tom is cleared out - Neck and crop. I got a new man named Osborne. He has a wife and 4 children in Sussex. He boards up at Mrs Dyer in the field - you remember her, she used to grunt. He saw me kill two bullocks and 4 sheep last week; that gave him an eye opener. He did 2 sheep himself on Friday, and did pretty well. Tom had got unbearable, did nothing, worse than ever. And what do you think I found after he had gone. He had actually pulled out the Copper in the wash house and sold it for old copper. That was a licker. I could not believe my own eyes. I saw him and told him he had to bring it back, but he said it was burnt out. The cheek of it. Now it will be the village cry - who stole the copper. He thought I was giving him 3 days notice, but he was wrong. That was a choker for him, I could see. He said he was living up in Niton and would come and kill a bullock for me if I wished. He thought he could not be done without, but thats where he made a mistake.*

April 10th - *I hope you will come and see me before you go out to stick the Germans. I have not heard from Tom, but I found he had had the Copper Hose off the old wooden calf bellows. He sold them, but I never got a penny. We had bad weather, nearly blowed our teeth out. It blowed down the big shrub by the slaughterhouse door and broke the grindstone, rather the stand, not the stone. Our old Terriers are gone; we have the Warwick's here now. They are much smarter looking. There's lots of changes in Niton. What a mess the Government is making of everything. Never makes up their mind, does things in half, look at it all. It is too much Party and Politics, instead of for Country and King. (What changes!)*

May 7th - *Nice to hear from you and that you were firm with that bloke. I see Lloyd George was down your way. He seems on the right track now, I really think he is genuine and means business. We forgive him for old times and slap him on the back for what he is doing now. How about Ireland. Pretty case of* pickles that, hey. Very short lived rebellion - Germany again! How about old Casement - hang him; shoot him, I say. I help pull out a Bullock, and some times not. I don't know how we will get on for exemption (up till then butchers were exempt from active service) Asquith's motto I suppose - Wait and See. We have to win this War and not keep it hanging about.

June 26th - Keep the men up to it. Give them a bit of what the Cat licks her tail with. You will lick them into shape. The loss of Lord Kitchener was the Nations loss, but thank God he had done so much for the Country before his end came. True, the German Fleet got more than they bargained for, but for the darkness and haze coming on they would have been wiped out. Well done our Navy. It is very sad about the Rayner boys being all gone, 3 from one family is very sad indeed. May often comes down and feasts her eyes on your photos. She would be as happy as a bird looking at one of them, makes her mouth water I can see. She's a plucky girl.

Aug 8th - Have you paid the Germans a visit yet; I am sure you would do your best and stick a few of them. We have not seen a Zeppelin over here yet. I believe really you would sooner be out there amongst the bullets. Now the Germans can see the red light. We had a nice beast from Chale Farm last week. We went for 2 but only got one home. The other tore up through Charles Dabell's place right back on the Down with the rest where he comes from. He is a rum one. You would like to be in it and kill the rascal tomorrow. They are good beasts but I don't like their temper and manners. The people should beseech the Almighty to grant us the victory over such wicked and blasphemous a Nation as Germany. That is my feeling and what I daily pray for.

Sept 28th - I am sure you would have liked to have helped with the Chale Farm bullocks. One was a rascal, Peach went after him in a Bullock Cart and then nearly lost him. He broke his cart and rope and nearly got away. We got him out and killed him at once. I'm glad you are crawling up, and 8d a day more pay, that's all right! May comes in and asks about you but she is interested in all Soldier lads now, and Sheep's Eyes is kitchen maid over Mr Prendergast.

Dec 18th - Glad to get a line, I had begun to wonder what had come of you. I thought you must be confined or something, I mean to Barracks, not with a baby. We are getting ready for Xmas. We are killing a good Devon Steer today, and 2 prize Down Sheep. I do not have much to do with the killing now. I killed 2 small steers last week, and a big one today. About the Government and the War, what price Lloyd George now. He kicked old Wait & See out and deserves a putty medal for doing it. I think now we will get on. I vote for Lloyd George now. You must see about getting ready for Berlin. It's not so far off as it was. I just heard there is a Cunard Liner ashore at Ladder Chine. I have not seen May for a long time, but Sheep's Eyes, and Florry ask after you.

1917

Jan 7th - *We got over Xmas very well, no candle light work. Everything was dressed nice and clean and looked well. The steer weighted 44-12, and one sheep 145lb and one 124lb, they were good and fat. We had the last piece for dinner today, it was lovely about two inches thick, but it was good. I saw May on Xmas Day and she asked for you, but I would not crush her hopes and longings with your message, so I let her hope and be happy. Ah, Lloyd George, he's the chap. He will bring us Victory, and I really believe 1917 will be the year of Victory. Not a comprimise but a real crushing victory on our terms. Pretty good cheek, Kaiser Bill offering us peace on his terms. Mrs Lang is postman in the village now. She owes me money and never comes near the place, and Mrs Russell nearly the same. They are a bad lot.*

Feb 19th - *Easter will soon be here, but it's no good now. The ration of 2½ lb a week has humbugged business, and the gentry have nothing. Several men from here have gone to be Soldiers, but we still have two men and a boy. Percy has taken to knock the bullocks down now, so you might guess he is a man too. Mr Prendergast is killing their own now. They have killed a Swan, and Rheuben's Donkey and have scarce anything from us now. Only a few ounces at a time. War ration. I expect they will kill Ruben next! The Swan was for soup, she was 18 years old, the Donkey for stews, he was 30. I have not seen Sheeps Eyes, or May for a long time. I suppose they are nursing the soldiers, they seem to have a pity for them. Its foggy here, we have not had any papers or mail for days. We do not know if Peace is declared, or Kaiser Bill sent to St.Helena. I want you to have a finger in the pie before its all over.*

May 4th - *Everything is change here these days. Everything turned topsy turvey. Did you hear that Miss Mortimer left her Domestic, Soloman £500 and a gold watch; Nile £500; the two Willis girls £500 each; Jim Baker £50; and Bert Hatcher £50; and other legacies. You can see all ways it's a case of Greasing the fat Cows Ass and letting the lean one burn. Ah, I forgot, May, dear May, she had £50 - she was a much younger hand. She is gone home to Cowes now. She came and saw me and is still interested in you and asked to be remembered to you. Poor old Nile has lost his wife since. No sense in anything here now, what with Rations and one thing and another makes life more or less a great humbug. But we are thankful to be in good health and busy. I think the Germans will soon be on the run. I am pleased the American's are taking a hand in the War with such good spirit and courage. Sheeps Eyes is interested to hear about you. I always tell her something nice about you, so you must feel something nice for her.*

July 6th - *I and everybody are about the same, including the young ladies. They often ask have I heard from Henry. I say Yes, and he sends his love to you. They smack their chops and go away very happy, easy way to cheer them up is it not. We are busy about nothing, yet a lot of work to do. Rations make small joints,*

One of many letters
from Mr Newnham
to Henry Roberts

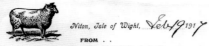

Niton, Isle of Wight, Feb 19 1917

FROM . .

J. NEWNHAM,
Family Butcher,
UNDERCLIFFE, NITON, I. of W.
ENGLISH MEAT ONLY.
FAMILIES WAITED ON DAILY FOR ORDERS.

Dear Henry,

I was pleased to get a line from you & to hear of your experience. Quite a treat for you. Easter will be here but it's no good now. The ration of 2½ lb per week has humbugged business. It makes such a difference with the Gentry, they have nothing now. Did you not wish you were going to France when you were at Folkestone. I should have went with him I think. You had a good trip any way. How remarkable to meet two Islanders on the journey. I sort of half know the two chaps you mean. It was fortunate you see across them. They must tee you a little. Dicks son Jack a soldier, went last Wednesday. Percy takes his place as Man Slaw for Chale and Nibees Charles, lets us Ny well & comes back safe. And we have the Saturday Eldridge Boy in Percy's place to work the undercliff. So you see we still have 2 Men & a Boy. Percy has taken to knock the spellers down now, so you might guess he is a Man

see forward

Continued

Why this is topsy turvey now, no sense in anything. Mr Holland has asked Westcliffe as a War Bargain. & who do you think bought it John Williams, as a spec. It will be a little fortune to him when the war is over as he bought it cheap as a spec.

Mr Prendergast is killing their own now. They have killed a swan & Rheubens Donkey & have scarce anything from us now. Only a few ounces at a time War rations. I expect they will kill Reuben next. The swan for Soup she was 18 years old. The Donkey for stew he was 38. Mrs Fords hair begins to curl already. I have not seen sheeps eyes or May for a long time, I suppose the are nursing the soldiers. They seem to have a pity for them. It is beastly foggy here to day have had no mails or papers since Saturday. So we do not know if Peace is declared or Kaiser Bill sent to St Helena. I want you to have a finger in the pie before it is all over. Trusting you are quite well.

Yours very sincerely J. Newnham

and more work. Now the Americans are in the War the Germans will begin to squeak. They are doomed and they are beginning to see it, and old Kaiser Bill's days are numbered. I should like to see more resolute Government in England. Look at the food constraints, does nothing. Prices are rising. The price of animals are risen out of all reason. Last week our Bullock cost over £60, rotten price, aint it. But nothing is done, and so it goes on. But with Beef and Mutton over 2/- a pound we must be thankful, and so we will be, and thank God we are still alive.

Aug 30th - So many young chaps are gone, I think of them all. But I recon its getting hot for Old Fritz now. I never loose heart. I would like to slap old Lloyd George on the back and say well done Lloyd George I never say bad things of him now. I curse all those blessed peace workers. I say make them fight or shoot them out of the way. Jim Baker made the splinters fly, had a weeks honeymoon. Good tune in the old fiddle yet, you see! We are busy now. We had two steers from Chale Farm this week. Pretty price too, 26/6d per score, and mutton 1/6½d per lb. I believe Sheeps Eyes is nearly tired of asking for you.

Oct 28th - You know Miss Saunders had a notice to look for another House, and that she was going to look at Grove Villa, but it was so black and desolate she could not do it. So we talked it over and I offered her to come and live with me. So, of course, to do that we must be married. We shall live together in my house. Now don't you think that a wise plan under the circumstances? I think you will approve of it.

Nov 1st - (Letter from M.Cawston, The Firs) - I am pleased you have heard of the forth coming wedding. Mr Newnham and Miss Saunders at last. I should think we shall all get some cheap joints the day before that comes off; I hope the first will be a son! All the old maids in the Undercliff will be looking up now thinking their turn is coming.

Nov 1st - (Letter from Mary Saunders) - I am quite sure it is the only and right thing to do, and I shall not have to work so hard, and I am sure we will be very happy. It will be very quiet such old fogies as we are. I knew the Niton gossips of course would have a hay day but it has been a nine-day wonder. Congratulations, Mr Newnham tells me you are engaged to Miss Sprake (note from Henry written in - "not quite - THR")

Dec 3rd - You know that a chap that goes courting has not much time for letter writing. I was pleased to hear your happy news. Poor Niton girls, I had not the heart to tell them, so let them hope on lest they die in despair. Poor May called and wished she could have kissed your dear fingers (crushed in an accident) to make them well, so I let her hope on, a pity to dash all her hopes. It would be cruel. You must think of us next Monday, Dec 10th at eleven o'clock at Niton Church, being married. Two Carriages from The Clarendon. Lunch at The Sandrock. Mrs Green will be Miss Saunders best woman, and John Willis my best man. So you see we have it all chalked and pretty smart.

Dec 17th - (Letter from Mary Newnham, née Saunders) - *Lots of people at the Church and they all said I looked very nice, also my husband Aheeeeee! We had such a happy day. Your father drove us in the coach and he put up white ribbons and we were pelted with rice and confetti.*

Soon after this Henry Roberts was sent to France, and did not bring back any more letters from his great friend, Mr Newnham. He returned safe and well in 1919, and spent the rest of his life in Chale, and married Octavia Sprake in 1922.

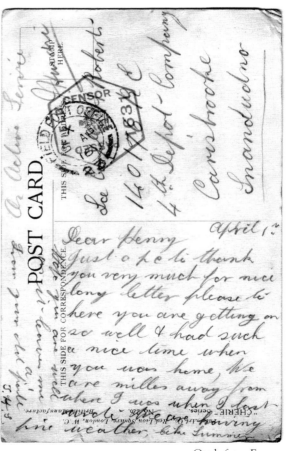

Cards from France

CHAPTER 8

HOME FOR GOOD; THANK THE LORD

After having spent over two years in the Royal Engineers, in Wales, training and then training others in the art of preparing trenches, building bridges and defences, etc. Henry Roberts was eventually sent to France, and landed there on 20th April (Easter Sunday) 1918. Many of his colleagues had gone before him, and many never returned, but possibly fortune smiled on Henry when he lost the top of two fingers in an accident, so delaying his departure to face the enemy.

After 11 months in France he returned to his native Chale, never to leave again (except for occasional visits to the mainland, and a return visit to Wales for his honeymoon). It was at this time that he started to write a diary, which he continued, on and off, for the next 40 years. Not being one to waste anything, the first records were kept in a 1911 Blackwoods Shilling Diary, still interleaved with blotting paper; Henry simply altered the dates to fit the 1919 calendar. Much of his words record everyday events of a hardworking farmer, gardener, and general worker in a simple village environment. But they reflect how a young man who had left our shores as a boy and who returned as a man, was able and prepared to throw himself into, and take a leading role, in village life.

The diary commences on Saturday, 15th February 1919 - (still in France). *"Paraded quarter to 11am and went through the DeLouser. Afterwards, moved up into what was called the 'Clean Camp' at Dieppe, but it was mud everywhere over your boot tops".*

The following day was a showery day in France. - *"After hanging about all day, we left the Concentration Camp at Dieppe and marched to the Docks from Martin-Eglise, about 3½ miles. We embarked at 21.00 hours on the 'SS St George' bound for BLIGHTY at last".* (Clear relief and joy in those brief words). *"I shall never forget the capers of a demobilisation journey".*

On Monday, 17th February - *"We found ourselves off Netley Hospital and we soon landed in Southampton, alongside the Mauretania. We had some rations on board, and in the Dock station. After being chased about like scalded cats from 2 o'clock to 6 o'clock we found ourselves DEMOBELISED. We left there at 6.30pm, and got down to Portsmouth, via Salisbury and Southampton by 9.30pm. Went to Miss Weston's Sailors Rest and had something to eat. Walked to Southsea Pier. Had a yarn (chat) with old 'Father Peter'. Came back to Portsmouth Harbour and slept in the Ladies Waiting Room until the Mail Boat started".*

Tuesday, 18th February 1919 was a rough day with snow in the morning. *"We left Portsmouth by Mail Boat, and came via Ryde to Newport, and arrived at 5.30am. Had a wash and shave in the Porter's Room at Newport Railway Station; the first I had had for three days. Telephoned from Market* (St James Square in Newport which was then the Cattle Market on Tuesdays) *to Chale, and Riddle and Octavia* (his brother and future wife) *came to meet me with the motor. Got hung up* (had an accident) *at corner of Lugley Street and St James Street with an ASC Lorry, and I put my arm through the glass screen, and we bent the front spring! Came home in Chiverton's motor, and mighty glad to get here. Thank the Lord it's <u>for</u> <u>good</u> after 11 months in France".*

The relief in those few words show just how Henry must have felt; perhaps like a release from a prison sentence for a crime he had not committed, but a job well done.

The next few days are recorded as going round and meeting his friends, and also going to a Concert in Niton where his brother *"Rid. sang two or three songs".*

On Friday, 21st February. - *Had a good 'Bust Up' in evening. We had about 30 here.* (In the Clarendon Hotel, his home) *Had a proper good evening, and I think everyone enjoyed theirselves.*

On his first Sunday home from the War, Henry went to Church three times. *"In the afternoon went to Atherfield to see the slip; a big bit gone right off the point just below the old Lifeboat Slipway".* Henry was home, and life was already getting back to normal.

The following day he started work around The Clarendon, which by the description of the jobs done, was in need of a lot of maintenance, having been allowed to run down during the War years. Clearly the carpentry skills Henry had learned were being put to good use!

On Tuesday, 4th March, 1919 Henry records *"Drew £8.14.3d Army pay from Post Office".* Against this date he wrote, *"Started this diary. Wonder how long it will last? THR".* Clearly the earlier entries were written up from memory.

Over the next weeks there was no shortage of work both around his home and around the village. The animals needed attention, and the buildings, but Henry was getting things into shape. Mr John Cooke the Schoolmater (who lived in the school opposite The Clarendon, and a long time family friend) asked him to do some jobs at the School. He records having caught *"eight mice and six little ones in a nest"* on one day, and *"some rabbits"* on another. On 18th March he *"fell down in Rectory Scullery"*

One entry states that *"Dad has been elected a member of Chale Parish Council"*, which drew the exclamation *"my stars"*! The Roberts were now well in with the local Community.

Friday, 21st March - *"I white washed the larder and the two places out back* (presumably these were the outside loos, but it would not have been spoken of in those days). *Percy Sprake* (the Carrier) *brought me a tin of bicycle oil from Newport, 1/- (5p)"*.

The following Tuesday *"Red heifer REDDIE fell down. We made a skid with the old donkey cart wheels and dragged her back into Rectory Yard. She is much better this evening; we drenched her with Vitalis, Whiskey, and Linseed Oil, and by the next day she was recovered!"*. And on Thursday *"Reddie slipped her calf this afternoon"*, clearly too much whiskey! Also, *"Fred Sturmey married for second time up Church. He's about 60 and his wife is 24 years"*.

References are regularly made to Dad taking 'gent indoors' to station, or to 'them indoors'. This was a reference of those vistors who were 'staying at The Clarendon Hotel', as opposed to the family, or the staff who lived or worked there.

On 31st March Henry records that *"I burnt out and scraped slop pail, and painted it white"*! He refers to *"had a go at paperhanging in No. 9"* (Room No 9 in the Hotel where he slept) adding *"mighty slow, but I must be thankful I can do it at all"*. He commented that he did it *"without fingers"*, and *"I miss my fingers and it takes longer to do it"*, reference to the loss of the tops of two fingers in the wartime accident.

On 5th April - *"Young Charlie Cheek* ('Boots' at The Clarendon) *brought Riddle a little dog fox about a fortnight old"* and then the next day, *"Peter* (the dog) *got in Oil house and killed little fox, so he's soon gone up shoot"*! There is also reference to *"bought some spuds called 'Carisbrooke Castle'"*, an old local variety of potatoes rarely grown these days.

As time moved on, Henry started to join in local activities, and on 16th April he *"went to choir practice* (at Church), *and was admitted to choir"*. And on Easter Day, 1919 he records that *"we all went to Church together for the first time for 4 or 5 years - last Easter Sunday I landed in France"*.

A few days later *"Old 'Diamond' had a cow calf without a tail right off close to the pin bone"*.

Henry learned through a list of names in the local newspaper that a T.H. Roberts of Chale had been awarded the MSM (Meritorious Service Medal), the first he had heard about his medal. A Major Hoskyn was 'indoors' at the time, and Henry got him to write a letter to the Army to find out if it was him. On 14th May he records in the diary that *"had a reply from Chatham to say I have got MSM"* and he commented *"Mrs Hoskyn sewed on the ribbon for me"*! One must assume the appropriate ribbon was sent ahead of the medal. It was not until 25th June 1919 that Henry made the journey to Yaverland Battery to be presented with his medal by a General. A very proud day.

Every day there were references to moving cows; mucking out stables; planting potatoes and other seeds; mending sheds and stables; and general work around the farm at the hotel. Dad and Riddle were busy with their taxi service for lots of people 'from indoors', including 'The Professor', and also for many of the wealthier people from the village.

One day he notes *"an old sow is ill - If a pig is unwell and wont eat, try them with an apple, they will eat that as soon as anything"*.

Saturday, 17th May 1919. - *"Went to meeting down Scout Hall about putting up Hymn Board in Church in memory of those who are killed"*. (The tense is in the present 'are killed'; they were still his friends). This Hymn Board still hangs above the pulpit in Chale Church, and is used to this day.

Tuesday 20th May 1919 refers to *"brought home pig from Wroxall* (Flux's Bacon Factory - they would have sent their pig there to be killed) *made into bacon, he weighed 12 score, plus the lard and face. Flux had the feet and pluck* (stomach), *and paid him 10/- (50p). We shan't go short of bacon now for a week or two!"* That evening he went with Octavia to an Organ Recital at Shorwell Church, and then went on to Brooke for a ride. *"Very nice evening"*.

Mackerel fishing had been a major occupation for the people of Chale for centuries, and on 1st June 1919 is recorded - *"First lot of Mackerel caught here this year; sold at 3 a shilling* (5p for three mackerel).

The Summer days saw life in the village slowly returning to normal, and a Sunday School Treat (party) was held at The Rectory. Henry took down some tables, etc. from the Hotel, and in the evening he went along - *"first time for years"*. He made 18lb butter.

By mid-June haymaking was underway. *"Started rueing in down Six Acres"*, and the next day *"went pooking with horse rake, and black horse 'Nigger'*. (Rueing-in is an old Isle of Wight dialect word for raking together swathes of cut grass into one row; pooking was putting the hay into piles ready for carting). *"Waggons came down at 10.00am, and we finished carting by 9.30pm, and I raked it all over afterwards"*. (There was little else to do in those days, other than work - no radio, no television, no videos). *"Char Parker* (his best friend from before the War) *came home from Scotland, brought me back 4 Curlews eggs; 2 Golden Pluvers eggs; 2 Peewits eggs; and 4 Sea Pilots* (Oyster Catchers) *eggs"*.

Next day Dad, with two nippers (boys) turned hay on Lower Ground, and started pooking up; I plucked the rick and put the sheet on".

On 29th June 1919 Henry *"went up to Obelisk* (the Hoy Monument), *and Pepper Box"* (the Pepper Pot, St Catherines Oratory, or the Chantry) both on St Catherines Down. *"Dad went to Sandown with the Band of Hope excursion".*

Haymaking - Tom Roberts on horse rake in centre

Friday, 4th July 1919 was a very good day! *"Drew £110.10/- for my hand* (compensation for loss of his fingers during the War). *In the evening went to Public Meeting down Scout Hall in connection with Peace Festivities, to be held on 19th July. £42 was collected, and they are to have tea, sports, and a Bonfire".* The following Thursday - *"Went up on Down furze cutting with Spanner* (Alfred Spanner, a respected local man) *for Bonfire".* This continued over the next few days, and the Scouts also helped pooking the *furze up".* On 14th July *"made up a dozen torches for on the Downs. To make torches, get some cotton rags and put some fat or grease inside and tie up in old wire netting, and pour on parafin!"*

Saturday, 19th July 1919 was Peace Day. *"Riddle and I got up 5.00am and decorated our front* (of the Hotel) *with flags. Poured with rain all afternoon. We had Peace Sports in Rectory field behind Bert Chiverton's house. I went in Pole and Bolster competition. There was tea for everyone in Chale Farm Barn, and the children had theirs in the Scout Hall. It was too wet and foggy in evening to have fireworks, so put off until Monday".*

Sunday - *"I am a bit stiff and tender after yesterday!"*

Monday - *"Still too foggy for fireworks and bonfire".*

Tuesday - *"Clear in afternoon. We had bonfire and fireworks on Down. Had 21 torches along the top; 10 facing Chale, and 10 facing Chale Green. Bonfire in centre, all burnt very well. Also had four 90lb Naval Flares - lit up all the Parish, could read by them down here! About 1 doz. hand lights, and eleven 1lb rockets, and thirty ½ lb rockets. It's the best show ever had on the Down!*

On 24th July Henry went to the Royal Agricultural Show, in the evening, the first show held since 1914.

A *"nearly nasty accident"* occurred on 6th August *"when I was raking down Rectory, the belly band* (part of the harness) *broke, the tug came undone, and the horse turned right round underneath the rake shafts"* Luckily nobody was hurt. *Five pigs were sent to Flux's, for £62; and they got three bundles of thatching spars from Matthews in Newport for 4/- (20p) a bundle. Jim White started thatching the rick.*

Henry records that he spent much of his time in the garden; doing carpentry work for friends and relatives; and working in the Clarendon Hotel for his mother, washing up; cleaning the silver; and other chores. Tom Roberts spent much of his time conveying people from 'indoors', and around the village, both in the motor car, or in horse drawn carriages.

On Sunday, 24th May 1919, Sir Sam Fay came to stay at The Clarendon until the Wednesday. He was to be a regular visitor 'indoors' over the coming years, later buying 'Northgrounds' near the Green. He was a wealthy train magnate who had taken control of the military and munitions train movements in England during the First World War. Sir Sam's chauffeur would sleep over the kitchen with Henry, or sometimes above the stables. The working class knew their place in those days.

A Sale of Work was held on 28th August in the Conservative Working Mens Club (now the Chale Women's Institute Village Hall). Henry noted that "Mother was weighed at the Sale - 10 st. 6lbs" (He did not say how much they got for her). Henry weighed in at 11st 2lb, and Bert Chiverton at 10st 5lb, but they were weighed in the Scouts Hall opposite. "Old Tom Mew came home from Canada"

Another near disaster occurred on 21st August when Miss Aldridge, who lived down The Terrace in Chale, gave her dog some pills and nearly poisoned it with strychnine. Henry cured the animal with ½ an egg cup of Linseed Oil.

The reputation of the Clarendon Hotel as the 'in place' to stay was further demonstrated when Sir Walter Napier and his family arrived 'indoors' on 2nd September. The next day Henry drove to Godshill and walked through Godshill Park to Wroxall, and saw Appledurcombe House (the ancestral home of the Worsley family). He noted in his diary - *"This is the first time I have ever been to Wroxall village"*!

A commotion occurred on 15th September when Annie Allen, a maid in the Hotel, *"went into hysterics last night and has been in daft ever since"*! Ridley, Henry's brother was demobilised *"at last"* and came home and *"he can continue his job as the Assistant Overseer for Chale"*. (This was an offical job looking after the poor of the village).

The following Saturday, 20th September 1919, Henry and his brother went on his motor bike to Fred Hollis's wedding; *"the first wedding in Shorwell Chapel. They were driven home in his wagon; four horses, and all decorated up. Looked fine. I reckon old Fred was well pleased!"*

The Autumn saw much time spent harvesting potatoes, and working indoors; driving the wagonette and even the Landau to weddings, etc.; and doing repair and decorating jobs around the village. Payment it would seem was 'optional'!

Tuesday, 21st October 1919 saw another major change in Chale life. At a special meeting "down Conservative Club", it was decided to turn it into a Social Club for the Parish. The name was changed from the Chale Conservative Working Mens Club to the Chale Village Club to make it more attractive to the whole community. *"I think it will be better"* recorded Henry.

The dreaded 'Foot and Mouth Disease' reached Chale around 22nd October 1919 when it was reported that George Bull's (at Gladices) cows had got the disease. There was an order out prohibiting all cattle from being on the roads. Henry records that *"Frank Pratt had just taken our cows down Military Road, so I went and fetched them back!"*. The disease spread around the village, and John Linington of Chale Green had his cows killed on 28th October; Tom Butchers at Presford Farm had to kill all his cows on 3rd November; and Morris's at Buck's Farm, Shorwell fell to the same fate on 7th November.

Henry records that on 24th October - *"I saw a queer bird down lawn with a long beak. Dad shot it and took it to Newport to get it stuffed, and it turned out to be a Woodcock, like a Curlew only it has short legs"*. The same day Henry started to learn bell ringing at Chale Church, a hobby he continued for many years. He commented *"hope I shall be able to keep it up"*. Henry was *"put on Committee for the new Social Club"*.

11th November 1919 was Armistice Day - *"All home together"*. *"There was two minutes silence for the Glorious Dead - there were 24 from Chale who perished. Everybody I think stopped, and I hope prayed - we did. I was made Treasurer for Club* (a position he held throughout its existence). *I hope it will be a success"*.

The next day they killed a pig, 11sc 6lb. Henry cleaned the chitlins (his spelling). Sid Cheek cut up the pig in the evening. Next day ½ the pig and both hams were sent to Lowers in Newport to be made into bacon. The rest was salted, and made 12½ lb lard, and some scraps. *"Helped catch Clara Rayner's cat. Heavy shower of snow in evening"*.

On 14th November they brought a 6' x 4' Billiards table to the Social Club from The Saeter, a large house near The Terrace. *"Went bell ringing in evening, got on better with it tonight."*

Over the next few weeks the Village Club was flourishing with Whist Drives, Dances, etc. There were over 40 people at one Whist Drive, and Ridley was the M.C. At this time Henry mentions several outings with Octavia, but she always took one of her sisters with her, although he always commented that they had a good time!

With Christmas approaching, on 10th December they *"killed big spotted sow out against big stable door down Granny's"* (the house known as 'Trills' next to Denhams). *"Oliver Chiverton 'Grumps' stuck her. Took her to John Brown's* (butchers shop on the Green). *In the afternoon helped John Brown kill Walter Woodford's pig in his garden* (next to Denhams), *and put it up in van"* The following day he *"went down at 8.00am to see the pig weighed; it was 22sc 1lb. He paid 28/- a score for him - £30.11.9d." "Had Dancing Class down Club in evening, about 50 there"*.

Throughout the diaries and letters, whenever a birth occurred it was always the father who had the child! On Sunday, 21st December 1919 *"Fred Sturmey aged sixty had a son and heir born at No 6 Terrace"*. (You will recall that old Fred married a young 24 year old girl on 27th March - he was just about within the time limit!!).

In those days, Christmas shopping and putting up the decorations were usually left until Christmas Eve. On 24th December 1919 Henry noted *"Went to Newport and bought some things for Christmas. Rid and I decorated up a bit in evening for Christmas"*. The following day, Christmas Day, Henry recalled *"My first Xmas home since 1914. Went to Church 7.00am, and I helped ring bells at all four services today, quite a record. Had five carols in the evening"*.

On 30th December *"about 30 cart loads of bank slipped across the road half way up Blythes Lane this afternoon"*

New Years Eve 1919 - *"Only four bellringers turned up to ring New Year in. About 20 people up Church Corner joined hands and sang Old Lang Syne. The Old Year finished up with a lovely fine moonlit evening."*

And the next day it was work as usual! So ended Henry's first year back home in Chale after his military service, and he was already taking an active role in village life.

CHAPTER 9

A NEW DECADE DAWNS

1920

And a new diary. This time for the right year, and a diary printed by Letts who were well known for their diaries, and a former Chale family. Members of the Letts family lived at one time in South View, one of the three large residences on the main Undercliff Road at Blackgang.

Henry Roberts' interest in Bellringing was growing, and he wrote in the first page of his new diary a short verse which was hung in the belfry of the Church of Tonge, in Shropshire, and written in 1694 by George Harrison.

If that to ring you do come here
    you must ring well with hand and eare,
Keep stroke of time and go not out
    or else you forfeet out of doubt.
Our law is so constructed here
    for every fault a jugg of beer.
If that you ring with spurr or hat
    a jugg of beer must pay for that
If that you take a rope in hand,
    these forfeits you must not withstand
Or if that you a bell O'er throw
    it must cost you sixpence ere you goe.
If in this place you swear or curse
    six pence to pay; pull out your purse
Come pat the Clerk, it is his fee
    for one that swears shall not goe free
These are laws old and are not new
    therefore the clerk must have his due.

The verse must have had an influence because on 2nd January 1920 he noted that he was gaining confidence with the bells. *"Getting better - never sweat"* he wrote. He is now ringing bell No 2, the oldest bell in the belfry, and a week later he is on No 4.

He also commented that *"Billiards and Dancing in the Club is also getting better!"*

Monday, 12th January saw the lifting of Foot and Mouth restrictions in Chale, which had lasted since 22nd October 1919.

The village social life was buoyant. On 13th January *"A Returned Soldiers and Sailors Dinner was held over School, about 120 present; went off very well. Then went down Scout Hall for Social, and over to the Club for a dance afterwards"*. On 16th January, Henry Roberts is re-elected Treasurer for the Village Club, and both he and Ridley were both put on the General, and Social, Committees. The following Monday a Whist Drive for Blind Soldiers was held in the Scouts Hall; there were nearly 60 people there and they took £4.

One of the most important decisions in the history of Chale was made on 20th January 1920. Henry wrote *"Had a Sports Committee Meeting down Scout Hall and we decided to have a Public Meeting about having a Flower Show"*. The Sports Committee had been running the annual Chale Sports Day for many years before the War, but this was the first attempt to hold a Flower, or Horticultural Show, in Chale.

There was clearly some curiosity about a visitor when, on 22nd January, he records *"Amongst the arrivals indoors was Mr Hetherington and his black Egyptian Valet; he has a lovely white Russian dog"*! The following day *"Riddle took 'Sinbad' the dark chap over Niton in the afternoon"*

Wednesday, 28th January 1920 - *"Large party of people went in Will Sprake's motor to Ryde to see the Pantomime 'Jack and the Beanstalk'. We got home about midnight"*. Riddle (who was an expert cook and chef) *"made a 4-tier iced cake for School youngsters tea party on Friday, which was held here. (in The Clarendon) There were 87 of them. After, they went down Scout Hall and had games and presents off the Christmas Tree"*. (This is another indication how, in those days, Christmas started on Christmas Eve, and went on through most of January, rather than starting in August and ending on Boxing Day, if the shops are anything to go by, as in the twenty first century).

Life was really getting back to normal, as, on 6th February Henry noted *"Tom Westmore cut my hair out behind Skittle Alley while we were on dung cart!"* Later they *"went down Ladder Chine and saved a tub of oil, and put it up in Whale Chine. Next morning before breakfast went down and emptied tub of oil into cans, and put it in another tub up top; then rolled the empty tub up cliff, and brought it home in the van"*. The fruits of the sea!

Another well supported group was the Girls Friendly Society, and they held a Concert *"down Scout Hall in evening. The place was packed full and the concert very good. Rid sang one or two songs and we collected £5.10/-"*.

19th February - *"Sports Committee Meeting in evening. Bruce Dabell appointed Secretary for the Flower Show"*.

The gardens were taking up much of Henry's time now, and there was great activity planting, hoeing, and preparing for the coming season, no doubt with the new Flower Show classes in mind. Many fruit trees were also planted.

Henry's friendship with Charlie Parker was further cemented when on 1st March *"I stood God-father for Charlie Parker's second son when he was Christened this afternoon - Walter Henry (after me!). Little bull had gripes in evening very bad. I drenched him and put hot bricks under his stomach"*.

Monday, 8th March - *"We were measured up for new blue serge suits at Fields in Ventnor, and they came today, £9 each. (very expensive for the time). The following Sunday it is recorded "Riddle and I wore new blue suits to Church for the first time"*.

Arnold Bros Fair arriving in Chale

Sometimes entertainment came to Chale, and on 16th March, *"Arnold's Fair and Pictures came down Chale Green in Percy Sprake's Perry Butt along Top Road"*. The following day *"went to Arnolds Pictures down Top Road"*.

In 1920 many villages and communities started erecting War Memorials to the memory of those who had fallen in the Great War. Chale was no exception, except that it was, in the Chale tradition, a labour of love, or perhaps duty to their departed school mates, that the young men of Chale who had returned safely erected the War Memorial themselves. On 11th March 1920 Henry noted *"George Bull, Walter Woodford, and Arthur Bull started putting in the foundations of the War Memorial in Churchyard. Dad took some stone down for it, and fetched some sand from pit"*.

On 12th June the base and cross arrived, and Henry was there to help unload it. The memorial was a standard design bought in from a mainland supplier. *"On 30th June helped with others to fix square block, and helped put stone up onto foundation. We all had a look at the bottom of the stone which very few in Chale saw* (I can only wonder what might have been on the bottom of that stone, but we shall never know!).

Dedication of Chale War Memorial 1920

SUNDAY, JULY 18th, 1920,

At 3·0 p.m.

✝

Dedication

OF THE

War Memorial

AT

CHALE,

BY THE

Bishop of Southampton.

On 2nd July - *"Helped fix the cross of the War Memorial in evening with four poles and an endless chain borrowed from Wheeler & Hurst of Newport. There were eleven of us helping. It went up beautiful, and everything worked splendid"*

The great day arrived - Sunday, 18th July 1920. *"The Bishop of Southampton came and dedicated our War Memorial* (note <u>our</u> memorial), *and consecrated the extension to the churchyard* (to the west side of the church). *Rid made a wreath out of roses from the lawn for the Memorial. Nearly everyone from the Parish present; we had a nice procession out of the Church to the Memorial, and back round to the new churchyard"*.

The Easter of 1920 proved busy for The Clarendon. *"We had 20 people indoors this Easter"*

12th March saw the first meeting of the Chale Parochial Church Council, with 10 people elected to the Council other than the Rector, Churchwardens, etc. Henry Roberts *"came top of the poll with 47 votes"*.

Major farm sales were now being held, so breaking up the old large farm estates all over the Isle of Wight. Henry records that he went to Newport for the sale of local farms. *"Chale Farm sold for £10,500, and Blythes (a field) for £50, to Fred Cheek; Atherfield Farm for £9,100 to Liningtons; Home Farm for £7,500 to A.E. Brown; and Dungewood to Morris for £5,800."* Henry bought a pair of Australian Brown boots from Mr Woodford for 30/6d.

A rare outing 'overseas' saw Henry and Hilton Cheek go to Reading Show on 2nd June 1920. *"We had to go to several places to find a bed; slept three in a bed and were charged 10/- each!"* (Henry does not say who the third one was!). *"Had three hours at the Show. Lots of cattle and machinery. We found a restaurant in Oxford Road called 'Clarendon'; it has been there for 30 years. Visited Newbury, and Winchester, and stayed three days!"*

By the end of July, excitement was growing for the first Chale Flower Show. On 26th July Henry went up to Blackgang and took 11 entries to Bruce Dabell, the Secretary. The judge for the Show was Mr C. Martin, the County Horticultural lecturer. Henry took him round to judge the gardens; 9 entered. While he was there, Henry *"showed Mr Martin my plumb and pear grafts. He told me Paraffin will kill blight on apple trees"*.

The first Thursday in August was traditionally the day of Chale Show for many years, and the first was held on Thursday, 5th August 1920 in Sid Cheek's field at Bramstone Farm, opposite the Methodist Chapel at Chapel Corner, where the Sports had been held before the War. Henry recorded *"Nearly 300 entries. Only had time to put in 7 entries, and got 3 third prizes. Took down four cabbages, two not for competition, the largest of*

Schedule of the First Chale Horticultural Show 1920

which weighed 25lbs and was as far across as I could reach! Everyone took up with big cabbage. I went in relay race with Char Parker". The event was clearly a great success, and continues to this day (albeit in a somewhat different form!).

10th August - "Mother paid me £10 for eleven weeks work".

17th August - "Took old Diamond (Jersey) and her calf to Market. She was 14 years old. It takes three hours to walk a cow to Newport". One wonders what the old cow was like by the time she had walked nine miles to Newport Market in three hours. "Young Charlie Cheek got in a paddy and nearly went in hysterics!" "Dad and I went up on Down with heavy cart and carted down a load of hay from Golf Links with the black horse. We had General Committee Meeting down Club, and I had young Gilbert Cox in for taking money out of billiard box."

Over the next few months there is a change in Henry's working patterns, and he starts taking 'stone' around to various houses for Dick Cox, the local builder. He noted he was paid £7.10/- for September carting. Time was spent ferreting, but not so much time working around the Hotel, or with the animals. He noted that, on 31st October "we had cold pheasant for tea".

Perhaps there was just a glint of 'straying' in Henry's eye around this time, as his diary refers on several occasions to "the new dancing instructor from Ventnor, Miss Harbour, who came down Club". "She seems to teach very well". On 4th November - "Dancing Class with lady instructor down Club in evening!"

The big world of finance caught up with Henry, when on 2nd November he noted that "Riddle took Miss Demetriadi (a wealthy 'indoors' lady) to Ventnor Station, and I took her luggage. When she got to the Station she was short of money and I gave her £2 for a cheque!"

On 3rd November there was a meeting of the Parochial Church Council with discussions about funeral expenses, and the rights of nonconformists regarding the Church. "Meeting was too long for Squire Way". (did he go to sleep?). Also, "squared up with Bert Chiverton down Club". (paid up the bills).

A Public Meeting of the Sports and Flower Show attracted a large gathering, and it was announced that they had £50 in hand, so it was voted to send £5 to Ryde Infirmary. Henry notes "I was placed on Tea Committee because I helped wash up last year". (There is a moral there somewhere!).

11th November 1920. - "Armistice Day. Stopped for two minutes silence in Cliff Acre opposite No 3 (No 3 The Terrace where his Aunt Patience had had her Guest House). Whist Drive down Club in *evening; I did the washing up!* He records that the Cenotaph in London was unveiled by the King, and the Unknown Warrier was buried in Westminster Abbey, on this day.

An indication that our weather was generally colder eighty years ago is shown in the amount of snow experienced. On 12th December *"it snowed all day and was about 6" deep. The cows had to sleep inside".*

On 18th December that year *"A large four-masted steamer, about 7,000 tons, the Edgar Luckenback ran onto the rocks just outside Lighthouse at 6.20am. She had a general cargo of grain, bound from New York to Rotterdam. The Government tug 'Sprite' pulled her off at high water about 3.30pm. Went over and saw her; straight out about 100 yards as you come down the road to South View Corner".*

Thursday, 23rd December - *"Sent off about 2 dozen Xmas Cards in evening".* (You knew they would be delivered the next day in time for Christmas).

Christmas Day - *"Went to Church, had five Carols. We had Mrs Slaters two children in kitchen for tea and made them a Xmas tree. Saw a Great Green Woodpecker down on lawn, feeding".*

29th December - *"Tasted some Sweet Wort down Corner"* (Henry was probably visiting Octavia Sprake, 'down Corner', and 'Sweet Wort' was a drink made from just Malt and water).

New Years Eve 1920 - *" 'The Old Year out & the New Year in'. I helped ring the Church bells at midnight for first time. I put No 1 bell 'up' to finish the old year, then the clock struck. Bert Chiverton, Walter Woodford, Fred Sturmey, and Fred Mew then got their bells up, and then we went on call changes for a bit. Then Alfred Spanner took a turn at No 1 bell for a time, and then they lowered. I hope next year we will be able to have them muffled, and go through all the changes"*

At the end of this diary Henry records his annual cash summary. Income £91.1.8d, Expenditure £37.5.8d, profit £53.16.0d. Over £1 per week, - good money! (I suppose it was all 'pocket money'; he would have lived free at home, and Mum and Dad would have bought his clothes; his work around the Clarendon Hotel would have been rewarded in other ways).

1921

With the arrival of another year, another diary. However, the entries become less regular, no doubt life for Henry was getting busier. On 14th January he mentions *"Had Scouts Supper here in evening".*

And on 8th April - "Eclipse of the Sun by Moon which we saw very plainly".

15th April - "*Railway men and Transport workers refuse to strike and leave miners to it. This will be called Labours 'Black' Friday. Snowed all day, and frost in evening. Covered my early potatoes with muckle*". (Muckle - Isle of Wight dialect for rotten straw).

The entry for 18th April reminisces that it was twelve years earlier in 1909 that Henry went to work for the local builder Dick Cox as an Apprentice at 2/6d (12p) per week. He also says "*I caught a lizard down Lowcliffe in a heap of stones; it was about 6" long and brown and spotted like an Adder.*"

7th May 1921 saw Henry ill, with his throat and face swollen. "*Called Dr Armstrong and he says I have influenza throat. He sent me some horrible concoction for me to take every four hours. I had great difficulty swallowing, even liquid, everything seemed to prefer going up my nose than down my throat*".

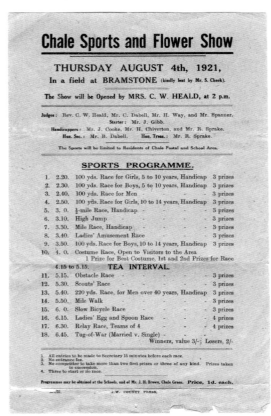

There was another ship ashore on 12th May. "*I heard a bang and after heard it was the Rocket, and there was a steam trawler bang on shore up South View. She is The Lewis, and is right on the old Essen at Rocken End*".

The 14th May saw Mackerel in Chale Bay for the first time that year. A few days later he records "*Frank Pratt flung a bucket of water over Charlie Cheek this morning - do him good.*"

On 26th July "*Took a pair of heavy cart wheels to Blacksmith to be cut and shet*". (I.W. dialect - to weld together as two pieces of iron), and the following Thursday "*Went to Brixton Show* (Brighstone) *in afternoon, but not much stuff there this year. Fred Hollis won greasy pole; he got across twice!*"

By 4th August it was Chale Flower Show day again. Henry had spent time putting up the tea tent; scrubbing the tables, etc. and he had taken some tables down to the show field from the Hotel. On the day itself he won eight prizes, and had won 16/6d. "*They had Tug of War, Marrieds versus Singles - Marrieds won 2 first pulls!*"

The summer of 1921 was good for business, and on 14th August The Clarendon had over 40 people in for tea extra to the residents, making 60 teas in all. Very busy.

On 10th September Chale played Brighstone at football down Parsonage ground, their first game, and Chale won 2-1.

Wednesday, 14th September 1921 *"Went ferreting up Combe. We had a proper good day, best we've had since War. It worked capital, and we caught 21 rabbits. Tinker* (a Jack Russell dog) *and Jack* (the sheepdog) *had a fight; could not part them until I stunned Tinker. He laid out about 10 minutes; I thought he was settled* (dead), *but he had nearly killed old Jack".*

The weekend of Friday and Saturday, 23rd and 24th September saw Henry off to the mainland again. *"Went for Choir Outing to Bournemouth, and came back through Salisbury Market. Went to the pictures down Cowes, came to Newport by the last train, and came home in John Brown's pony trap".*

5th November *"Did not have a bonfire or fireworks. I did a bit up in Maids room"* (I assume he means he did some decorating in the Maid's room?).

There were always rewards from the sea, and that Autumn saw a lot of driftwood come ashore. By 29th November Henry says *"Have got up last of wood from shore. Pulled it up from Whale Chine. Also pulled up 2 sheets of iron from The Cormorant* (a wreck some years before) *from bottom of Whale Chine for Edgar Linington to make a bridge".* *"I caught Edgar and Bruce Dabell ferreting Sandbury, and along upper hedge at Combe, so I went and told them they had no business there; they made out they did not know!!"*

On 30th November Henry's mother Grace Roberts went on holiday to London and Leeds (her home town) *"the first time she has been on a holiday since she was married"*, in 1892.

8th December *"Went to Whist Drive, about 50 there. I washed up."*

On 11th December Henry noted that *"Went ringing down Church. Mr Spanner said to me 'They poke you about anywhere, don't they', and Mr Woodford says 'Yes, he's the handiest one we've got for that!"*

A tragedy happened on 20th December 1921. *"Poor little 'Tinker', Riddles white dog, got run over down King Hall* (the stretch of road from Sweet Briars to Scout Hall corner - the field here is also called 'King Hall') *by Miss Watkins of Ventnor. They were very upset* (and so I expect was poor Tinker). *Buried him down garden next day".*

On 27th December - *"Lost two ferrets up Spring Hill. Went down next day to find them, but could not find any trace of 'em. Went back after dinner with some paraffin and tried to smoke them out. Could not make anything of that so started digging on speck. After half an hour I found the young one, but could not catch her until I had dug about as much again, before twas then nearly dark so I dug to the end of the hole hoping to find the other one, but instead I found three more branch holes and was as far from the end as ever, and had to give up as it was too dark".*

29th December - *"Roused young Charlie Cheek round because he flung down some water in back kitchen; made him chuck down a lot more and then wipe the lot up!"*

Saturday, 31st December 1921 - *"New Year Eve. Rung the Old Year out, and the New Year in, and had the bells ½ muffled. Did it in fine style going bang through the 120 twice without a blunder. This was the first time I have done it, and the others hadn't done it since 1916".*

CHAPTER 10

BETWEEN THE WARS - VILLAGE SOCIETIES, MARRIAGE, AND A SON

Horses on the farm - Chale Church behind

As the work got harder, the number of diary entries lessened, but Henry still kept notes of the important events in his life.

20th January 1922 - *"Dad shot old dog 'Jack' up Six Acres"*.

26th January - *"Albert Stallard (Blind 'Dad') died at Blackhouse aged 75 years"*.

7th February - *"Broke cow stable window walking backwards with strips of wood"*!

3rd March - *"Went bellringing; went through about 30 changes when my bellrope broke and came right down. Bert Chiverton and I went up and spliced it, put the splice inside the wheel; then we went on again and had a good practice afterwards"*.

8th March - *"Rough day. Very heavy wind, hardest ever known. Blew off several slates; the elm tree, and the big elder blown down. Blew a slate across onto Church roof and broke some of the tiles above the porch. Went painting indoors, finished about mid-night"*.

18th March - *"Chale drew 1 each with Godshill at football"*.

29th March - *"Ada (the maid in The Clarendon) fell off the chair steps outside Lunch Room window and broke them"*. (But, how was poor old Ada?)

15th April - *"Planted 10 varieties of Sweet Peas"*.

5th June - "*Gentle, the crumple horn cow got hung with two strands of barbed wire inside her horn to Ted's fence up top of Mead; we had a job to get it out*".

12th June - "*Cut my left thumb with the heal of the reap hook; nearly took a slice off, only hung in the nail*".

29th July - "*Tom Westmore cut my hair out in field*".

3rd August - "*Show Day. Took down some chairs and piano from Scout House. Helped in tea tent in afternoon. 540 entries, and we did over 700 teas! I had 1 first, 4 2nds, and 6 3rds*".

12th September - "*Tom Westmore found old Alf Butcher* (Blast) *dead in bed this morning so he is not coming to work today*". (It is not clear if it is Alf or Tom who is not coming into work!)

14th September - "*Went to Ventnor to have my suit fitted. Bought pair of black boots, and two white shirts.* (No doubt all for his forthcoming wedding to Octavia). *Took old gentleman and two ladies indoors for drive*".

Henry and Octavia Roberts married - 18th October 1922
Tom Roberts; Alice Sprake; Ridley Roberts (best man).
(Name unknown); Grace Roberts; Henry and Octavia; Oscar Sprake.
Joyce and Olive Sprake (bridesmaids).

21st September - "*George Downton married Milly Douse at Kingston Church. I drove her to church; went right up in the field by the Church big-gate with the carriage. Dad sent me with the pair, 'Pat' and the black horse 'Nigger', this is the first time he has ever trusted me to take a pair of horses, and had the best Landau, quite a record*".

18th October 1922 - HIS WEDDING DAY (No entry in the diary, and no comments on the honeymoon!)

18th December - *"Came down Denhams to live, Octavia and I"*. (The house was then owned by Grace Roberts, Henry's mother, and they lived there as her tenant until she died in 1939).

22nd December - *" 'Dapper' my little black and tan long tailed pup that I got from Char Parker was going down with me and was running along in front of the van when Mrs Young's dog jumped out through the gate and frightened him and he stopped short right in front of the front wheel and I went bang over him both wheels and killed him dead on the spot. I would not have done it for ever so. He was a real good pup and would have made a splendid dog; but there tis done and thats it. I had the hump all day"*.

26th December - *Buried 'Dapper' down garden next to 'Tinker'*.

29th December - *Octavia and I made the butter.*

1923

21st January - *"Went up home to dinner, and down home to tea. Came back in time to ring bells"*. ('up home' was to The Clarendon, Henry's former home; 'down home' was to Westmoretown, Town Lane, Octavia's former home).

9th April - *"Caught a dozen mice under the corn bins with Peter and the little kitten. The kitten had four in its mouth all at once"*.

4th May - *"Old Gentle got her crumpled horn hung up in Uncle Ted's barb wire again this evening"*.

2nd November - *"Walter Brown,* (from the Chale shop and bakery), *fell down dead up in bakehouse this morning about ½ past nine just as he was washing his hands. Policeman Fay, Dad, Riddel and I carried him indoors afterwards"*. Tuesday, 6th November - *"..buried Walter Brown in afternoon"*.

....

Whilst Henry continued to keep his diary for many years, the entries are mainly routine. However life went on much as before until on 1st February 1924 Octavia gave birth to two premature babies, both weighing less than 2½ lb each. One, named James Roberts only survived for 30 minutes before passing into God's arms. The other, named Thomas Edward (and always known as Edward to his family) survived. In an effort to assist the expectant mother, Octavia's niece, Mabel Nicholson, the daughter of her sister Harriett, was despatched from Grantham to 'Denhams'. She provided support to the Roberts family, in many ways, for the rest of little Edward's life. During the Second World

War she did her War Service by working on the farm at Denhams, whilst Edward was in the Army.

So fragile was Edward at birth that he was christened at the bedside, as was James, and spent the first few weeks literally wrapped in Cotton Wool. It was 10 months later that he was strong enough to go out, and a pram was purchased. He lived to the age of 80 years.

Edward Roberts went at first to Chale School opposite his home where he had his early education, but in 1937, when 13 years old, he went to Newport Grammar School, a private school in Newport, where he spent the last three years of his school life. He excelled at Religious Knowledge, and History, which were both to play such an important role in his future life. It was at school where he gained knowledge and a lifetime's interest in the 'Wild West', and throughout his life he read numerous books from the Mobile Library which visited Chale weekly, and collected books on the North American continent. This was possibly due to his curiosity in wishing to find out where his Grandfather, Mary Roberts' husband and the father of Tom Roberts, had gone when he went to New York and never returned.

Following the ending of his schooling, Edward worked for his father on the farm until called up for Army Service in 1943.

Henry and Octavia Roberts, with Edward

Edward Roberts, aged 10, at Chale School - 1934 (second from right, front row)

114

Between the two Wars, Henry and Octavia took an ever increasing involvement in village events and activities, many centred around The Clarendon Hotel and the two Halls, the Village Club and the Scouts' Hall.

ST ANDREW'S CHURCH, CHALE

The Church of St. Andrew's had always been the centre of their lives, and Henry was elected to the newly formed Parochial Church Council, and became its Treasurer at a time which saw many changes in everyday life. Electricity came to Upper Chale in the 1930s and electric light replaced oil lights in the Church, and the Church Organ also benefited from this new facility.

THE CHALE BULL SOCIETY

But farming was their living, and when The Chale Bull Society was formed, both Tom and Henry Roberts joined. In 1920 the Ministry of Agriculture and Fisheries introduced a scheme to encourage improvement in cattle breeding, with the provision of grants to Bull Societies. Basically, the Government gave a grant to properly constituted local Bull Societies to encourage the improvement of the breed of cattle in the district by provision of a high class bull or bulls.

Chale Bull Society receipt

The Society could either buy a suitable bull, or arrange with an owner of a suitable bull to place the animal at the disposal of the Society, for use by its members. A grant of one-third of the purchase price, or its estimated value, up to a maximum of £20, was paid to the Society. Members had also to contribute to the cost of the bull, and to pay stud fees and costs of running the Society.

This was an opportunity to gain access to high quality bulls, and so improve the breeding stock of cows, which otherwise they might not have been able to afford. With many small farmers with just a very small number of cows, the cost of keeping a quality bull was not viable, but through the Society all could improve their stock. This was before the introduction of A.I.

Henry kept Guernsey cows, and this breed, through the English Guernsey Cattle Society, became popular in Chale between the wars and the availability of a suitable Guernsey Bull in Chale would have encouraged others to keep this breed. From records here the production of butter was an important part of their farm work and this breed is well known for milk with high butterfats needed for quality butter. The in-season cow would be walked to the farm where the Society's bull was kept, such as to Hawthorn Dairy on the Green where Mr Newnham kept the animal, and the act was performed. The Secretary of Chale Bull Society was the recently retired schoolmaster, John Cooke. He had to keep records for submission to the Ministry, as well as minutes, accounts, etc. for which he was entitled to receive a maximum of £2 per annum for each Bull in the scheme. A meagre sum for such an important role!

How long the Chale Bull Society survived is not known, but as with others, the Roberts were forerunners in many things in Chale, and clearly supported the scheme.

CHALE VILLAGE CLUB

Chale & District Working Men's Conservative Club 1911

The building which is now known as the Chale Women's Institute (Village) Hall started it's life as the curiously named Chale and District Working Men's Conservative Club, in March 1911. The land on which it stands was part of Chale Farm, and was leased to the Club. A number of philanthropic local gentlemen, presumably with a view to encourage the working class to vote Conservative, and at the same time provide them with a club where they would organise their own activities, raised the money to build. Shares in the venture (although not set up as a Limited Company) were offered at £5 each, and this attracted sufficient funds to build the Hall which externally has altered little over the years. Interest was paid annually.

After the Great War, there was a need to provide a more general centre for village life, and on 17th November 1919, the name was changed to the Chale Village Club. Henry Roberts was appointed its first Treasurer, and remained as such until it was eventually handed over to the Chale Women's Institute in 1953. The account books covering the whole of this period were kept intact by Henry, and survive to this day. They

Chale & District Village Club 1919   The Conservative Club/The Village Club - now Chale W. I. Hall

also contain signatures of others who can rightly be regarded as 'Men of Chale', who audited the accounts annually and who signed them as such - Robert Pinnock; Alfred Spanner; Harold Linington; J. Harris; Dennis DeLacey; and Tom Sprake. An autograph book of more 'Men of Chale' in itself!

Right from the start of the Village Club income flowed from Whist Drives, Dancing Classes, and Billiards; and also from the sale of lemonade, recorded under the heading of 'Amusements'. No alcohol there! Newspapers were provided for members to read (today it is the internet and wide-screen television which would be provided), in 1919 everyone relied on the newspaper for the latest information. Some were sold to members. The caretaker, and the Secretary (Herbert Chiverton) were rewarded for their efforts. Fred Cheek, owner of Chale Farm, received £1 per annun in Ground Rent.

In February 1933 the Club purchased the land on which their Hall stood from Fred Cheek, for £35.0.0d. Over the following years both income and expenses varied greatly as the popularity of the Club changed. Maintenance and general repairs were undertaken regularly, for which we must be grateful to this day. Electricity was installed at a cost of £7.7.0d. in April 1935, a wireless was purchased in 1936 from P. Bye for £21.7.0d. At the same time the piano was sold for £1.0.0d.

In September 1938 a fete was held jointly with the Women's Institute, raising £17.5.0d. for each. The war years brought almost a stop to activities, but the Club had to pay 11/- twice a year to the Inland Revenue for War Damage Contribution. In July 1942, in an attempt to keep the Club 'out of the red', £2.10.0d. was donated by the W.I., and in January 1943 £5 was received from the sale of the billiard table. Almost all activities ceased after March 1940, until January 1944, when Socials, Whist Drives, and income from Billiards re-commenced. One must assume that whilst the billiard table was sold to raise funds, it stayed there until after the War.

Alan Barton took over as Secretary, and in September 1951 a bequest of £100 was received from the estate of the late Sir Frederick Eley (of the cartridge manufacturers, who lived as South View, Blackgang). This enabled the Club to purchase a second-hand Billiard Table from the Old Comrades Club in Yarmouth, for £35.00, and it was transported from there and assembled in the Club by Les Chiverton the local Carrier, for which he charged £10.12.6d.

In March 1953 the Chale Village Club Hall was given to the Chale Women's Institute, in whose ownership it remains to this day. They also received the balance of funds, some £74.9.3d. Those involved remember going into the Hall and having to fight their way through a mass of cobwebs; the cloth of the Billiard Table was moth-eaten; and the building needed a complete overhaul, but it was saved for the people of Chale. Henry Roberts was still Treasurer to the end.

CHALE WOMEN'S INSTITUTE

Whilst Henry did not join, his wife certainly did! Meetings were held in the Scouts' Hall between the Wars, and some in The Clarendon Hotel during WW2. The Women's Institute movement started in Canada, and in 1915 spread to England, and is probably the reason why their Chairman is known as a President. An Isle of Wight Federation was formed to support local branches in villages all over the Island, under their motto "For Home and Country". In 1926 a

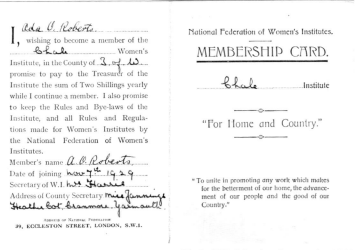

Chale W.I. Membership card - 1929

press report indicated there were over four thousand branches nationally with a membership of a quarter of a million ladies; it was described as 'the most important body formed during the century', and the State had subsidised it to the tune of £50,000! Chale formed an Institute around 1926, and Octavia Roberts was a member in 1929 when the annual subscription was just 2/-d. (10p). She, and many of her family, remained loyal to the W.I. for the rest of their lives.

THE BLACKGANG LANDSLIDES OF 1928

We have come to accept the seemingly unstoppable landslides along the south-west corner of the Island as inevitable. Indeed, without them the Undercliffe, from Ventnor to Blackgang would not have existed. The fact that this area was considered one of the most beautiful areas on the Isle of Wight, some say in Great Britain, was due to massive earth movements some five million years ago. And yet they have continued almost continuously off and on ever since.

When a huge landslip occurred in the Summer of 1928, blocking the main road from Niton to Blackgang for ever, it was both the loss of the beauty of the views at the famous part of the road known as Windy Corner, and Big Rock, and the loss of a convenient highway, which shocked the population. The road was the last linking these two places, where once there were at least two; possibly more. The journey to Chale now had to be made using the inland route through Chale Green, until a new road was built.

Signs in the area had warned of the risk of a major landslide for some time before, but the main slip started in mid-July with a huge fall of part of the cliff face, and produced a slow slide of rock and mud affecting an area of some 20 acres of land. Daily, and almost hourly, the scene changed as the ground slid towards the sea, taking the road with it. Further falls followed. News of the landslides produced national interest, with newspapers reporting that most of the Isle of Wight was about to disappear into the sea, causing much consternation for relatives of local residents who feared for their safety.

The landslide at Blackgang July 1928

Few people had telephones and the first indication of the disaster was from the press.

The effect on the population, and business in Chale must have been considerable, but as usual it was an ill wind. Thousands of people visited the area to see the Landslide, as it became known. It was in the Summer and the Island was full of visitors, and the approach roads, from both the Niton, and Chale sides became blocked. Parked cars stretched all the way to Chale Rectory from where the passengers walked to Blackgang to see the disaster, many having to walk past The Clarendon where, no doubt, the Roberts took advantage of the situation; probably again on the return journey when after a two mile walk there and back, they were in need of some refreshment!

The largest numbers came on the Sunday, and by Monday it was reported that the whole area appeared like a well attended fair! People were climbing all over the moving mass, in spite of warning notices (the best way to attract attention is to put up a notice 'Keep Out"!), and picture postcards of the falls were already on sale at the scene for visitors to send to relatives and friends. H.R.H. Princess Beatrice, the Island's Governor, with Princess Helena, made a detour to view the Landslip for herself, and

The second landslide at Blackgang Sept 1928

during Cowes Week when making her annual visit to Blackgang Chine, Queen Mary, possibly with King George V, viewed the scene. A further, even larger fall occurred in September 1928 when a part of the overhanging rear cliff fell, ending for ever the chance of reopening the old road.

There have arguably been larger falls in the vicinity both before and after, often taking dwellings and other buildings with it, and the downward 'slide' continues to this day. As one who climbed over the barriers and past the 'No Entry' signs following the major slip in the 1970s, it must surely be like being in an earthquake with the ground below your feet clearly moving, and groaning as it slides uncontrollably seawards; the former road split and turned at right angles to its former route; and buildings sunk deep into the chasms which had opened below them.

Blackgang was now left as a cul-de-sac from Chale Church, and all chance of reopening the old Blackgang Road was soon abandoned. A new road, to become known as 'The New Road' was eventually built over the Down, through the Chale Golf Course, and opened around 1933, relinking Niton and Chale. The roundabout created along its length above Blackgang was constructed in the 1980s when the encroaching cliff edge made the previous road into Blackgang impassable. Life in Chale

The New Road from Chale to Niton opened 1933

soon adjusted to the new highway and the convenient if not so picturesque road soon became accepted by the local population. But arguably, local businesses benefited!

....

CERTIFICATES AND HONOURS

Appreciation for services rendered, and awards received were traditionally marked by the presentation of beautifully coloured certificates. As a just reward for many roles by Henry and Octavia Roberts, and young Edward, they received certificates.

Henry was the Branch Treasurer of Chale Branch of the British Legion (not to gain the accolade 'Royal' until many years later), from its formation in 1924 to 1944, and received an illuminated certificate 'as a mark of esteem and appreciation of his work as Hon Treasurer'. This was signed by Bruce Dabell as Branch President and Fred Mew as Branch Chairman. In a letter from the Branch Secretary, E.Eade, he thanks Henry for his work for the branch - *"No one could have done more"*.

Henry was a Special Constable for a number of years. He also served as a School Manager of Chale School.

ISLE OF WIGHT
SPECIAL CONSTABULARY.

The Bearer Thomas H. Roberts
is a member of the above Force.

H. G. ADAMS CONNOR, Captain,
CHIEF CONSTABLE,
NEWPORT, I.W.

This Certificate is awarded to

Thomas Henry Roberts

as a mark of esteem and appreciation of his work as *Hon Treasurer* of the *Chale I of W* Branch from *1924* to *1944*.

A. B. Dabell. Branch President.

F. Snow. Branch Chairman.

R. Rede. Branch Secretary.

Henry Roberts was the founder Treasurer

Henry was for many years involved with the National Savings Movement, and on its 21st Anniversary in 1937 he received a certificate stating that 'The National Savings Committee gratefully records its appreciation of the services generously rendered to the National Savings Movement by T.H. Roberts'. This included collecting savings from the pupils at Chale School, who on purchase of a National Savings Certificate through the scheme received a back-dated certificate granting them an interest bonus on their savings.

NATIONAL SAVINGS MOVEMENT

PATRON, HIS MAJESTY THE KING

TWENTY FIRST ANNIVERSARY
1937

THE NATIONAL SAVINGS COMMITTEE
GRATEFULLY RECORDS ITS APPRECIATION
OF THE SERVICES GENEROUSLY RENDERED
TO THE NATIONAL SAVINGS MOVEMENT
BY

T. H. Roberts, Esq.

PRESIDENT

CHAIRMAN

NOWELL EDWARDS

Henry Roberts organised the movement in Chale

The receipt of certificates started whilst Henry was himself at school in Chale, and in 1906 he received a certificate for 'Annual Written Examination in Religious Knowledge', signed by the Rector, Rev. C.W. Heald.

Edward, however, received a Certificate which might have had some concerns for his parents, both of whom came from families in the Licensed Trade. When aged ten, in June 1934, he gained a

Certificate of Merit, First Class, from the Hampshire and Isle of Wight Band of Hope Union - Awarded for excellence in Reporting a Lecture on 'Alcohol and the Human Body'. Whatever Edward learned was not of any lasting consequence in his later life!

President of the British Red Cross Society.

Grand Prior of the Order of St. John of Jerusalem in England.

Presented

by the Joint Committee of the British Red Cross Society and the Order of St. John of Jerusalem in England to

Miss Ada O. Sprake.

in recognition of valuable services rendered during the War.

Countersigned

Secretary.

1914 – 1919.

83, Pall Mall, London.

Chairman.

Vice Chairman.

Recognition of Octavia Sprake's War Service

As Octavia Sprake, Henry's wife received a ten year medal from the British Red Cross Society, and at least two certificates for her work during the Great War. This service was regarded as War Service, as much as that of any soldier, and she served as a Red Cross nurse at "Underwath", near Ventnor. She was able to contribute to the War effort in the best way she could.

And just one further certificate which the Roberts family kept safe for some 75 years, was a certificate awarded to Chale for gaining Second Prize for the Parish Exhibit in 1927 at The Great Autumn Fruit & Vegetable Exhibition held by the Isle of Wight Horticultural Association 'for the encouragement of food production in the Isle of Wight'. Henry contributed to the success of the Chale exhibit.

Chale Village exhibit at IW Horticultural Society Show 1925

ISLE OF WIGHT COUNTY COUNCIL.

EDUCATION COMMITTEE.

INSTRUCTION IN

HORTICULTURE

A COURSE OF

SIX LECTURES

WILL BE GIVEN AT

CHALE,

IN THE

C.E. SCHOOL,

BY

MR. C. MARTIN, F.R.H.S., M.H.E.A.

(County Horticultural Instructor),

Beginning on Tuesday Evening, Oct. 14th, 1930,

At 7 o'clock, and continuing on the following dates :

Tuesday, November 11th, 1930,   Tuesday, December 9th, 1930,
Tuesday, January 20th, 1931,   Tuesday, February 17th, 1931,
Tuesday, March 17th, 1931.

ADMISSION WILL BE FREE, and the Agricultural Education Sub-Committee cordially invite the attendance of all persons interested.

County Hall,
   Newport, I.W.   H. JERVIS, M.A.,
      September, 1930.   Director of Education.

J. W. JACOBS, PRINTER, CROSS STREET, NEWPORT, I.W.

CHAPTER 11

'UP CORNER', OR,
A HALF OF SPRACK'S OLD

The marriage of Henry Roberts to Octavia Sprake in 1922 brought together two Chale families who had been associates and friends for many years, although the Sprake family had been in Chale far longer. One family were blacksmiths, farmers, and now hoteliers; the other fishermen, smugglers, and brewers. The fact that they lived at the two ends of the village helped to draw Chale together; and become linked through a marriage.

The Star Brewery c. 1890

The Sprake family were Mackerel fisherman from the late 1700s having their boathouse on the slightly higher ground near to the shore, at the foot of Ladder Chine, in Chale Bay, and it was 'down Ladder' which was the location of many of their early escapades. Ladder Chine is a wind blown chine (as opposed to other chines in the area which were formed by streams draining off the nearby fields, and cutting a deep gorge to the sea). Situated between Whale Chine (which until the stranding of a 63ft

Whale at the foot of the Chine in 1758 was known as 'Mackerel Rail', presumably because of the nets which would be hung up to dry on rails there) and Walpan Chine. Chale Bay Mackerel became much sought after, and considered the best fish to be had anywhere off the Island's coast. Mackerel is a fish which must be eaten quickly after being caught, and the arrival of a shoal in the Bay was a much prized catch, prompting the quick despatch to local towns where the cry 'Chale Bay Mackerel' was greated with much enthusiasm.

Catches of four, five or even six thousand fish were not unusual, so the arrival of the first shoals in mid-May each year brought much interest from everyone, including the children, who were allowed to leave school to help with the catch. It brought its reward to all who were involved. With boats at Blackgang (mainly Wheelers); at Ladder (Sprake); and Atherfield, it really was 'first come, first served'. A signal would be sent from a look-out man on the cliff top to the waiting crew on the shore below once a shoal was sighted, and the first crew to get the signal and launch a boat would get the catch. They would row out in a clinker-built boat, paying out a rope held on the beach attached to a seine net which in turn was shot around the shoal and back ashore. Helpers would assist in pulling in the net, and when close to the beach, they would get behind the net to ease the catch onto the shore, getting soaked in the process.

The presence of mackerel boats, either used as rowing boats with several oars, or when the weather permitted, as sailing boats, meant that the crew members were skilled sailors. Their knowledge of local waters enabled them to cross the English Channel to such as Barfleur on the Normandy peninsula in France, presenting them with ample opportunities for involvement in the smuggling trade.

But that is another story, as they say!

By 1804, Robert Sprake is recorded as having built houses in Chale, and it is highly probable that he was responsible for the building of at least one of the cottages at the top end of Town Lane, near to where the boundary between the Parishes of Chale and Shorwell meet. The earliest was probably a small single storey cottage on the roadside, near to the parish boundary stone and which gave it its early name of 'Bound Stone Cottage'. Just to the rear of this, a slightly larger four-roomed cottage was built, and aptly named 'Corner Cottage'. It was here that Robert Sprake was living by 1822, and possibly earlier. Later these two cottages were joined, with the area in-between becoming the Bar area.

He was married in 1818 to Elizabeth Williams, whose parents were also to reside with them. By evidence of writing in books and documents, she and her brother Edward Williams had had a fine education in the late 1700s, and were most literate, which stood them well in the running of a business.

Initially, a Mr Stephen Lake and Robert Sprake had what was described as "a Market Garden" on the site, each owning adjacent plots, and Lake was living in Bound Stone Cottage. The venture failed which may have contributed to the setting up of a brewery utilising a ready source of spring and well water, albeit the buildings were on the higher ground in the area. Exactly how or why the brewery started is unknown, but brewing was common in country districts, and many farms had their own brewhouse, using their own barley, and farm workers were paid partly in beer. Indeed, the Island word of 'Nammet', usually associated now with a snack in mid-morning whilst at work, was originally linked to a meal of bread and cheese, and a drink of stronger beer, known as the Nammet beer, around 4.00pm whilst working in the fields, to take them through to perhaps 7 or 8 o'clock in the evening in summer months.

However, the close links with the Cross Channel trade no doubt added to the success of the project, and with the granting of licenses in 1833 to Robert Sprake, not only to brew beer, but to sell wines, spirits, tobacco, snuff, perry etc. presented an opportunity too good to miss. The smuggled brandy could be sold over the bar, with a licence!

ROBERT SPRAKE, LICENSED BREWER,

CHALE, ISLE OF WIGHT.

FAMILIES SUPPLIED WITH GOOD AND PURE
HOME-BREWED ALES
Of every required strength, delivered in casks of any size, at all parts of the Island.

PALE BITTER ALE.

The founder of the Star Brewery 1833

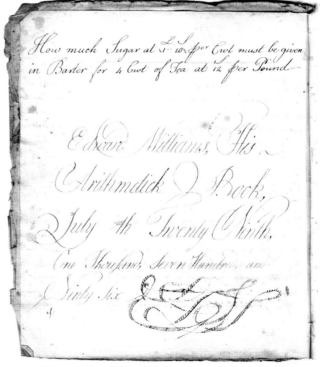

Extracts from Edward William's Arithmatik book - 1796

The success of the venture and the expansion of the brewing, and the failure of Lake's market gardening venture, led to an upper floor being built in brick above the stone lower walls of Bound Stone Cottage and by the 1860s this was the brew house. It continued to be used as such until 1922 when the higher brick building to the rear, along the Top Road side, was built. The brewery was named The Star Brewery, and the public bar, The Star Inn.

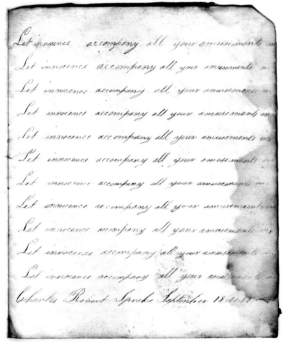

Extract from school book of Charles Robert Sprake 1832

On Robert Sprake's death in 1865, the licence passed to his eldest son, Charles Robert Sprake, and his four children, Charles, Oscar, Alice Agnes, and Robert were each brought into the business on leaving school. As evidenced by their numerous school books from Chale School, and also by their father's school books which were from an era before the present day School was built in 1843, the family were all well educated.

Charles was drowned in 1873 when having taken Mackerel to Freshwater in a boat known as 'The Spider', which had been heavily tarred over the years and was somewhat unstable. On the return journey off Compton the sail got stick up the mast. In an effort to free it, one of the three crew, Alfred Spanner who lived next to the Star Brewery in Town Lane, climbed the mast and upset the boat. All were thrown into the sea, but whilst the other two were able to keep a hold on the vessel, Charlie was lost.

Charlie was the head brewer at the time and was held in high regard, due partly to an incident some years previously when as a teenager, being on the shore when a cargo of brandy had been landed, and he was raking over the marks of the boat and footprints in the shingle, he was approached by some Coastguards. When asked if he had seen anyone that evening he relied 'Yes', and directed them up the beach, in the wrong direction, so saving the family from capture!

Both Charlie, who was married with three young children, and his brother Oscar, lived at Westmoretown House in Town Lane which had been the property of Oscar's wife Mealah's father,

William Chiverton, an Army pensioner. Oscar took over his brother's role as brewer, and later held the Licence until his death, being known to all as 'The Guv'nor'. In memory of his elder brother, a barrel of beer from his last brew was kept, sealed. Over the years it was only tapped on very special family occasions such as a christening, when Charlie's health was drunk; a hole being drilled in the tub and a wine glassful only was removed, the hole being bunged-up again. They added a small amount of beer from each subsequent first brew of the season (which was considered the best) to keep the tub full. Over the years its strength made it almost undrinkable, but it was considered an honour to taste this liquid.

Receipt for beer from The Star Brewery 1874

Knowledge of this tub became well known across the Isle of Wight, and stories of drinking a pint of 'Sprack's Old' as it was known from Charlie's last brew drew many customers to The Star Inn. Even 50 years later they were still selling half pints of 'Old', much to the delight of their customers, who would wait whilst the barmaid would go out of sight to draw off some stronger beer from a tub at the rear of the brewery, saying that there was just enough left this time! It never ran out! (It was something like the parable of the loaves and the fishes!!).

Oscar Sprake and his wife, Mealah, had eight daughters, several of whom took an active role in the brewery. The youngest daughter, named Ada Octavia (as the eighth daughter), was to marry Henry Roberts in 1922. The brewery passed through the hands of several of the Sprake family, but following the death of Oscar in 1926, and problems with sustaining both a supply of water and the disposal of waste water following a venture into bottled beer in 1924, it was sold to the Portsmouth brewers, Brickwoods in 1928. They continued to brew beer there until 1933 when the brewery closed, just 100 years after the first licence was granted to Robert Sprake.

Oscar Sprake's card c.1920

The Brewery, at Harvest time

Advertisement - 1905

The beer was an Ale, described as being brewed from Malt and Hops only, and at 'any required price'. There was in fact just one brew, and the variation in strength, and the resultant price, was achieved by adding a little extra water! The Star Brewery owned or served Pubs and Clubs all over the Island, and gained a reputation of the 'best' beer around. They had a Cooper, and made their own barrels in various sizes. The waste products left following the brewing process were sold to local farmers as fertiliser, and this resulted in Hops growing in the hedgerows in the district, and are still common here to this day.

Being a 'tied-house' to Mew Langton's, The Clarendon Hotel was unable to sell Chale Ale from the Star Brewery over its bar; also there is no evidence of smuggling being organised from there. However, as is mentioned elsewhere, following the death of Tom Roberts in 1943, several of Oscar Sprake's daughters helped run the Bar at The Clarendon. The link between the two premises was at last established.

Oscar Sprake could also rightly be called a grand old 'Man of Chale'.

A busy day at Sprake's Brewery c. 1925

Bottle label c. 1925

Oscar Sprake - 'The Guv'ner'

Returning home after a happy day

Edward Roberts 1943

CHAPTER 12

I'M IN THE ARMY NOW!

Since leaving School, Edward Roberts had worked on the farm at Denhams, with his father, but by late 1942 having attained the age of 18 years, the inevitable call came to serve his King and Country in the struggle against Nazi Germany. Edward wanted to join the Navy; his love of the sea and his interest in the Navy drew him to the Senior Service, but for some reason he could not do so. And so, on 7th January 1943, he was to join the Territorial Army to become a driver, as T/14510943 Roberts. Never having driven anything other than a horse, and some cows, this was a fitting choice for his army service!

Just as his father and mother had done when Henry had served in WW1, weekly, and at times, daily letters between 'Mam' (as he always called his Mother) and Dad and young Edward, kept them and him, informed of what was going on, and again many of these letters were kept to provide a record of their thoughts and fears. The following selection tell their own story, and how life in Chale was affected, and continued, by the effects of War. Omitted are frequent references to local men who were reported wounded or killed, and as the War progressed, these became a major part of almost every letter, to a point where they became almost routine, but nonetheless, tinged with great sadness and concern for their grieving parents left behind.

Edward Roberts, in uniform, with Mam and Dad.

Having never left home without his family before, the young Edward must have set out for Towyn, in Wales, where he was enlisted, in some trepidation. Almost following in his fathers footsteps. No doubt the fear of the unknown, and a pang of homesickness (although he never admitted it) set in on the first journey, alone. On the way he wrote a card home:-

8th January 1943 - *I am writing this on the train near Aberdovey. The Ventnor train went to Cowes and I was supposed to change at Sandown, and I did not know it and so had to go to Newport and I missed the boat across. I got to Waterloo at 12.15pm, and then I got the 10.50pm train from Euston to Crewe. I am alright and still got some of my sandwiches. Don't worry, Edward.*

A letter followed, also dated 8th January, to Mam and Dad. *When I left Ventnor I did not know that I had to change at Sandown; the Porter did not shout it out until my train had started off for Cowes, via Newport. I had to go to Newport and got the next train to Ryde; I missed the boat, but got the next one and got a train to Waterloo. Then I went by tube to Euston. It was a straight journey.* (No doubt he had been looking at the London Underground map - it's all straight lines!) *I had to wait about 10 hours for the train to Crewe and spent the time in the station as it was wet outside. I saw Poles, Norwegians, Yanks, including a Nigger, and a lot of Canadian Officers and men, and a lot of Naval officers as well as sailors. A policeman told me I could not use the YMCA as I was not in uniform. I was a bit worried at first because I missed the train, but I soon got over that and dozed a bit in the station waiting hall. I slept on the train up here.*

When I got out we were met by a Lieutenant and were taken to a hut where we were given a card with our name and number on it, and we had to tie this on our jackets. Then we were taken to get our bedding and blankets (straw mattress). When they knew my initials were T.E. they asked if I was Tom, and they said they would call me Tom even though you call me Edward at home. We had sausage and porridge for breakfast. Then I got my kit - two pair boots, and 1 slipper for gym; four pair socks; 4 shirts; 3 battledress suits; razor; hair and boot brushes; tooth brush; some soap and some underclothes. This afternoon we had to change into uniform, and we were inoculated. My arm aches a bit, and I am excused duty for 48 hours. I think I shall like it here! Edward.

12th January - from Edward. *I have not worn my pyjamas yet as the first night I did not take off my clothes as my arm was stiff from the inoculation, so I will send them back with my other civies and my case. My suit has got all creased. Please send me plenty of rags for cleaning equipment; and some dusters for wrapping up boot brushes, etc.; and I should like a couple of small boot brushes for brushing mud from leggings. I like it here; there are some nice chaps. We had a couple of shots with the rifle the other day; I shot a bit too high. The next day we fired three rounds with a bren. That is a better gun to aim with. I had three teeth out this afternoon. We will be here about six weeks, then if we pass we will be posted to a Regiment.*

18th January - from Mam. *How did you feel when you first got into your battle dress; like a trussed up chicken? Don't worry about your suit, but don't you think you better keep your pyjamas? I will send some dusters tomorrow.*

18th January - from Edward. *We get 21/- (£1.05p) a week; they stop about a shilling (5p) a week for Army Charities. I got 10/- (50p) worth of National Savings Stamps at the Pay Table, and when I get a book full I will send them home for you to get Certificates with. I have not touched last weeks pay and I think I shall be able to buy a £1 worth of stamps next week. We get lots of food, and I think I am filling out by the way my belt fits. Some got told off for not having their buttons shone up properly, but the Captain pointed mine out as been really shone properly; I clean them with 'Soldiers Friend' like Dad said he used. I could not get any at first, and tried Brasso, but that's no good. Please send some black 'Wren' boot polish and some apples when you next send a parcel. I am sending you my vest and pants and shirt to wash.*

20th January - from Mam. *I hope you like the cakes. The bag with your clothes arrived this morning, but are you keeping back your vest and pants, and grey socks, as I did not find them in the bag. We heard that Commander L. and the Doctor, and all who went in the ship with them are all gone down.* (This refers to the 'Fidelity' - see Chapter 13). *There was someone came out by bus to The Clarendon asking where the Commando's bungalow was and he said they were all missing, and he had to sort out his affairs.*

24th January - from Mam. *I was going round with the milk in the afternoon and got up as far as School. There was a rumble like thunder and machine gunning the other side of the Down, so thought there was a Raider about. It was the other side of the town where they came last time. There were a few killed, and I think Knights Library up the top of the High Street came in for it this time, besides other shops.* Our machines brought one of them down. (The details are kept 'vague' in case the letter gets into enemy hands - the town was Ventnor. Edward would have known this from the building mentioned). *We have got an old push pram and we have had a box put on it to carry the bottles in, so that will make it much more easy for us.*

25th January - from Mam. *Glad to hear you are getting on alright. I could not get you any black Wren Boot polish, only brown. How do you get on about washing your clothes. Dad used Soldiers Friend; he says don't put much on, but polish well. We have got our milk trolley; it was brought up yesterday. Mabel and I used it this morning to deliver all round here, and down Terrace. It holds 30 pint bottles. I will send you some Kiwi Boot Polish tomorrow, with some apples and the rags and the brush you asked for.*

27th January - from Dad. *I am glad you managed to find your way alright. I am glad you clean your things properly as it makes a lot of difference. Soldiers Friend is good stuff, but do not put too much on, and brush it in well. I am glad you have got all your teeth done.* (Edward kept all the teeth in a box for the rest of his life!). *We are getting on well. Mam and Mabel* (Edward's cousin who took his place working on the farm) *go off in their 'Chariot' to Terrace and back in no time. Mabel helps me out in the stable just like you used to do, and then she goes up Upper Houses with the milk, on her own. I finish milking and then go* to Blackgang with the milk. The ferrets got out last evening and the old one came round to the back door at once, but I did not find the little one until Monday morning when she came round back door too. Bob has pecked all the Emmet (ants) heaps and little thorns out.

The milk 'chariot'

29th January - from Edward. I have been 'Spud Bashing'; not a punishment, but the others went on a Route March and it was raining hard when they left. They said they enjoyed it; I wish I could have gone. And today we have been crawling on damp ground, but we didn't mind that; it's better than 'Square Bashing'.

9th February - from Mam. Dad has been to Market and bought a cow, and had to pay £60 for it and a bull calf; it's a lot of money, but we need the milk. Send me any of your clothes you want washed.

11th February - from Mam. We are getting on alright delivering the milk. What do you think Dad brought back in a milk bottle this morning; he left a bottle at Puckles and forgot to get it on his way back. A big mouse had got in it and could not get out; he looked very happy in his glass trap! Dad took it in to show Grandad; he is a little better today.

15th February - from Mam. I will send you the County Presses when I send your clothes. I suppose you wash your socks and handkerchiefs. The new cow seems alright. Dad named her 'Topper' as she was the top price in Market. 'Ladybird' has had her calf. Mabel and I were busy last Friday morning. There were some soldiers all along the road from Church Corner down to here, hiding behind the hedges, and several came in (at The Clarendon) and asked if we could fry them some sausages. They had the fat to fry them in with them, and some wanted cocoa made, so they had a good feed under the veranda on the table, and Aunt Lil was busy making tea. The Land Army got up a Social last Thursday for Mrs Churchill's Fund, and Mabel won the box of groceries.

22nd February - from Mam. I expect you were surprised being put as a driver; I suppose they are wanting drivers badly.

PS - from Dad. Remember what I said to you when I said good-bye -
          "Be sure the words are true,
          God has a plan for every man,
          And he has one for you" (and that's to be a driver!!)
We are getting on well with the new cow, and we have plenty of milk now.

1st March - from Mam. *How are you getting on with the driving?   I cannot imagine you at that job! You asked if the fowls were laying, well, we have only got three left. Mabel went down a fortnight ago and found some dead in the field with feathers all over the place, so we think the fox must have had them. The Hounds met at Chale Green yesterday, so lets hope they got him. We saw in the Mirror of the loss of HMS Fidelity. Mabel has been to see the Noel Coward film 'In which we serve'. We listened to Mr Churchill's broadcast this evening. He is a wonderful man. I have not received your washing yet.*

14th March - from Mam. *Next week we will have to go to the Post Office and collect our papers. The boy said they were short handed so they will not be able to deliver. Dad is going to apply to the Agricultural Committee to do the ploughing up; he has got all Six Acres manured, and is getting it spread next week.*

26th March - from Mam. *Do you want another towel sent; shall I send the one you used to take to Camp. You must let me know about the vests; have they got too tight for you?*

1st April - from Mam. *I have sent you some ginger cakes and some apples. They have started doing the threshing today. There were ten men to help. They have done the Wheat rick, and will do the Oats tomorrow. They got 22 sacks of wheat, and Fisk & Fisher will take the lot. Grandad* (Tom Roberts) *is not very grand. Well it's time for bed, Dad and Mabel have already gone up.*

11th April - from Mam. *We had another raid this week, Wednesday morning about 7.30 when they came over the Market Town* (code for Newport), *and did a lot of damage. Jordan & Stanley's shop in Node Hill was burned down; Wooldridge's pork shop, and Phillips drapers shop are all gone, and others damaged. Ruth Burt's husband was killed whilst working at Morey's* (timber yard). *Dr. Stratton and their maid was killed and his wife seriously injured under the ruins of their house. Pyle Street; Node Hill; and the bottom of the High Street got it most.*

August Hill (the name of a field) *is ploughed and worked down. We had a roller, a disc and spring harrow fastened behind each other onto the tractor. They are hoping to drill Oats tomorrow. We still have several loads of Mangels left down Church Ground. The Rape that was in the Mangels looks like turnips gone to seed, and as high as your shoulders; we are using that up for the cows. The Hungry Gap is higher than your knees and looks like a big bed of Parsley. We have been listening to the Queen's speach on the wireless; she spoke well.*

2nd May - from Mam. *We were surpised you measured 2 inches more round the chest in the time. I expect you have put on a little more weight as well. Have you used up all the butter yet? Grandad seems to be failing. Dad put the horses on the Spring Tine Harrow with the pair of horse reins and harrowed Butt, and it is ready to put in the potatoes. Dick came and shod Dandy* (the farm horse).

9th May - from Mam. *The doctor came and saw Grandad and told us he did not think a lot of him. He said he had a stroke and we must not be surpised if he went off in a sleep. We have got some ducks from Mr Brown at Niton, a dozen brown ones. Send your washing if you got any for me to do, not let it get too bad!*

13th May - from Mam. *Grandad gets very restless at times, and the doctor says he could linger on for some time. Shall I send your vest and pants, and would you like those gloves. Mabel will post this tomorrow when she takes the cows up. Last Thursday afternoon some Jerry's was over; the Cinema you used to go to was damaged, and some killed and injured.*

19th May - from Mam. *Glad you were able to go to Edinburgh. I sent your vest and pants off by the morning post, and I put in the chocolate and some sweets. Grandad is not so well; sleeps a lot. George Hardy is a daddy, he has a son born down his mothers. Several of us went to see the film 'Desert Victory' at Ventnor; they have opened up the old picture place, 'The Gaiety'. They had a special 'Youth Service' up Church; it was Youth Sunday, and the anniversary of the Home Guard.*

22nd May - from Mam. *Grandad passed peacefully away about 3 o'clock this morning. We were expecting it.* (The end of an era).

30th May - from Mam. *It was nice and fine for the funeral. Everything went off very well. There were a nice lot at Church. We had a Cross like we had for Grandma, and we put some roses off the lawn through the middle. There was one wreath the shape of a horses collar. We don't know what will come of The Clarendon; they can't get Ridley out until 12 months next September unless they arrange with him.; it is something to do with the Lease. They cannot give teas for a time as the Catering Licence has expired and they did not know, so at present there is only the Bar work. It seems strange up there now.*

There is some news! Mrs Robertson, you remember, the Commando's Doctor's wife, is come to be District Nurse. We were pleased when we heard she was appointed. Dad says the Mangels are coming up down Cricket Field, and a man has been out to inspect the white clover field for a seed certificate. The Growmore Club walked round Atherfield Farm last Thursday.

5th June - from Mam. *I have not received your vest and pants yet. We had the raiders over Wednesday morning; done a good deal of damage at the next village (Niton). 3 or 4 were killed but not anyone you know. Several houses were damaged; Osborne's, Dr Barker's, the Hotel down under his place had a direct hit but there was no one there at the time. The children was all in school, and the bombs dropped near, but the children were not hurt.*

Uncle Ridley has been over school (Chale School) cooking the dinners for the children as Jean had to register and is now on the land. They advertised for a Cook in the County Press but have not got one yet so Uncle has taken over for a time.

11th June - from Mam. *We start our Wings for Victory Week (a charity to support the RAF in bombing raids on Germany) on Monday. We are having a Miniature Fete at The Clarendon. They are having a few races and a produce stall, a White Elephant, and a Whist Drive Social in the evening at Scouts Hall. I think our target is £600. Mabel sends her best wishes. She is getting on well and can milk all the cows now, except 'Topper' and 'Blossom'.*

16th June - from Mam. *I got your washing on Monday and will send it back on Friday. Don't wear your pants so long another time, they need so much washing to get them clean. The Fete went well; we all helped with the teas, and the washing up. Dad got out the old Rocking Horse and the children enjoyed that, and we had a raffle of one of Uncle Ridley's rugs that he made (Ridley Roberts was famous for making beautiful woollen rugs some of which are still in use to this day). With the Social in the evening we made over £50, and there is a Whist Drive tomorrow evening.*

The Clarendon's old rocking horse
(with young Edward)

22nd June - from Mam. *I hope you are getting on well with your swimming, you always wanted to learn. We did well for the Wings for Victory, our target was £630, and we got £2,190 so we were well above it. (In a press report at the time it was recorded that the £630 was the cost of a four-engined bomber raid on Berlin. It also records that by 1943, War Savings credited to Chale amounted to £11,659). I was going to send you some strawberries, but I did not know if they would travel well; I will send you some Gooseberries when they get ripe. I forgot to ask you, have you had your trousers altered yet? We have had a busy day, what with hay making, butter making, etc.*

28th June - from Mam. *Dad went down Terrace and asked the Officer about having some of the soldiers to help him up here. He sent up 8 men; they came about 6 o'clock in the evening, and stayed until 9 o'clock.*

They pooked it up ready for carting the next evening. They had Dandy and the trolley, and got on very well. They were only young chaps about your age, and had joined up since you. The soldiers gave a film show - 'The Next of Kin' and 'Mickey Mouse' down Scout Hall tonight. Those who went said it was very good; they also gave a show last Thursday, but we did not go as we were too busy haymaking.

15th July - from Mam. I will send your vest on; and Aunt Lil has made you a Sponge Bag out of a Gas Mask bag she had, so I will send them both soon. Dad is getting ready for the machine. (Milking Machine).

25th July - from Mam. They have not finished the milking machine yet. The electric light man came last week and connected the wire and brought it across the road, and they have not been since.

3rd August - from Mam. The Land Army got up some sports yesterday like they did last August Monday, for the Red Cross, and the Prisoners of War. They had a good time, and a Social in the evening. Mabel won a knitted cushion, and Dad won a ladies jumper, and a turban that Mrs Horsley knitted to get money for the Lifeboat Institute and District Nursing Fund. The electric light man has been today to finish off the milking machine, so we are expecting the man to come in a few days and rig it up. I wonder if you can get me some brown paper; being a soldier they may let you have some, and I need some for the parcels. Young Greville has gone to join up today in the Air Force.

10th August - from Mam. The Milking Machine man arrived at about 1 o'clock today. He is sleeping up Clarendon and having his meals there. It was unpacked and washed with hot water and fixed up, and the cows were milked with it this afternoon. The cows behaved very well except 'Jessie', and she would not give it down very well, but the others did not seem to mind it. Several others are interested in how it works and they are thinking of having one. Have you got your new trousers yet. I will not send your vest and pants until I know you are settled in. (Henry Roberts was clearly a pioneer with the Milking Machine in Chale. Later he went back to hand milking!)

18th August - from Mam. The Milking Machine seems to be going on alright. It doesn't look as if we will get over to the mainland now, there is a ban on and you cannot go without getting a permit. It was a bit noisy here last Wednesday night with Jerry paying us a visit. Dropped two or three (bombs) in very good places on the Downs round, but did not do any damage, The news has been good this week; we seem to be pushing forward. (The army). I have put some chocolate in the parcel, and some apples.

8th September - from Mam. Did you hear the good news at 6 o'clock this evening that the Italians had surrendered; the best news of the War as yet. We have been carting the Barley all day, and they were all pleased when Dad went out after the News, and told them. He has been helping Mabel clean the Milking

Machine. *They take it all apart and wash it once a week, so that is a Wednesday evening job. There was a Gymkhana at Ryde last Saturday, and Mr Sampson and Mr Dabell went in the event for the open jumping competition. They took two of Douglas Dabell's horses he keeps up Brick Hill; Mr Sampson rode one and won it and got the cup and pretty pleased it had come to Chale.*

10th October - from Mam. (Edward had been home on leave) *I hope you got back in time, and did not have too noisy a time in London. The cows have behaved themselves, and Dandy, and the Wagonette is going on alright. I am sending your gloves tomorrow, and Mr Warder (the village cobbler) will call and take your boots to be mended. We have just heard by wireless that Mr Churchill is back from the USA and Canada.*

10th October - from Edward. *Thank you for sending the sweets and gloves; please send some rags as soon as you can. I shall be glad to get my boots as soon as they are ready. You can send my vest and pants as soon as you like, and I will send the dirty ones back when the others arrive as I have no brown paper.*

15th October - from Mam. *I am still waiting for your boots, but will send them on when they are done, with some rags. Dad has gone up the Hut (ARP) tonight on duty.*

PS. *Your boots have just arrived; I will send them on.*

19th October - from Mam. *I am sending your boots off today. Mr Warder has put some rubber soles on them, and said they should wear better.*

24th October - from Mam. *Dad went over Niton this morning for an ARP practice; it had been postponed last Sunday as it was wet!*

30th October - from Mam. *I am sending some County Presses. I have marked the piece about Uffa Fox's Parachute Lifeboats. (A wartime invention by Uffa Fox who had a cottage at Lowcliffe, Chale). We are still short of milk. Dad got some National Butter from Wray's in Newport; he sent in to the Food Office and they gave him a permit.*

7th November - from Mam. *There are a lot down with the flue. Aunt Mab has been helping delivering the milk in the pram.*

28th November - from Mam. *I got Arthur (Arthur Sprake, the Carrier) to get me a scarf at Newport and I have marked your initials on it and it is ready to send once I have your new address.*

.

5th December - from Mam. *I sent you some apples, chocolate, and some County Presses so you will have something to read. I hope you will like the scarf and find it warm. You said you have a long and short sleeved vest; would you like me to send you another long sleeve one, and have you got one of those Balacklara Caps* (her spelling!). *Mabel will be back to work soon, it is a month since she was took bad. Our wireless H.T.* (high tension) *Battery is gone and they don't think they can get us another before Christmas; we have not been able to have any news for a month now. Dad has just gone up ARP Hut; it is his turn on.*

12th December - from Mam. *It has been very cold and we have had some snow, and I think there is more to come. I have been thinking of wearing your red night-cap on my Blackgang journey. I have not made any Christmas Puddings yet as they have not got any fruit in shop, but I am hoping to get some this week. I broke my glasses when I dropped them and they say they will not be done for a fortnight, so I am using a pair of Aunt Mab's.*

16th December - from Mam. *I have not received the photos yet, or your vest and pants.*

19th December - from Dad. *Mam goes to Blackgang delivering the milk with Frank* (Pratt) *and Dandy, and Mabel goes down Terrace, while I stop home and feed the cows. I have fixed up the grindstone on the old butter churn stand and it does very well. I am sorry to say the fox got into the ducks a few nights ago and finished them off, all except one, so I killed that as it was hurt. May God Bless you and take care of you my dear boy. Your loving Dad.*

Then Mam wrote at the end. *I have sent you a cake, I hope it won't be too dry. I have sent a silk handkerchief which you can put inside your coat collar to save the rub, it would be softer. May 1944 bring us Victory.*

December 1943 - from Tom Sprake (Edward's Uncle, and a former brewer). *I somehow thinks that this War with Hitler is going to be over within the next six months. I don't think they can stick the bombing they are having lately. It's a pity they could not pitch one on Hitler and his gang and blow them all to ALE?*

PS. Must try and catch a rabbit for Christmas Dinner.

1944

14th January - from Mam. *We had the Sunday School tea up Clarendon today, and we have had a lot of soldiers in for tea. They are staying at Scout Hall tonight.*

20th January - from Mam. *You will be sorry to hear that Douglas Dabell's big horse that won the Cup that Mr Sampson rode, is dead. When we went up to Blackgang he was in the field and was nearly done for, and when we came back he was dead, and Biles' lorry was there to take him off; he was got old.*

30th January - from Mam. *Send me your vest and pants as soon as you can. Have a Happy Birthday (1st February). I cannot think that you are 20, makes me feel quite old.*

- from Mabel. *Here's wishing you a Happy Birthday. Grace has had a nasty abscess in her face but it is now emptying itself; they are nasty painful things. I know your Mam is disappointed she has not got a cake for you, but we will be thinking of you.*

- from Dad. *We had an alarm up Hut from 9 to 11 pm, and another from 3.45 to 5.50 next morning. I saw them get one in the lights in the evening and pass it all along as if it was in the box of a big wheel. (A German plane). Have a Happy Birthday.*

6th February - from Mam. *Dad went to John Chiverton's funeral. Last Thursday evening the Home Guard were having instructions on a machine gun in their hut when a live round got in with the dummies and struck John Chiverton in the groin and he died almost at once; and Philip Bullock was hit in the stomach and taken off to Ryde Hospital and is in a rather grave way. There was a lot at the Church; it was a Military Funeral. The Home Guard, and the A.R.P. were in uniform. Dad helped dig the grave. I am sorry you lost your purse; was it the one with the zip fastener? I will send you another one. We are very short of milk, but 'Minnie' calved this morning so we should be better in a few days.*

There is a gap in the letters kept, possibly due to the impending training for D-Day, or that they were not kept, however, on 19th July 1944, Mam wrote to Edward. *Frank Pratt has gone to Gurnard; they say he got there alright. Uncle Ridley (who was now running The Clarendon) came down just now and asked me to go up and be Barmaid with Aunt Lil tomorrow evening. (This would not have been such a problem as both sisters had helped run the Star Inn when their father had the Brewery there). I think they will miss Frank - he took his rations for a fortnight. We have not had any dido's with that Heifer up Blythes since!*

Edward was shortly to take part in the D-Day landings; his training in the Army was complete. He was now a proper soldier!

Chale looking south

Chale looking north

CHAPTER 13

TWO EVENTS THAT SHOOK CHALE IN WW2

HMS Fidelity

No story of Chale would be complete without a reference to the 'Commandos' as they were known locally, and the ship H.M.S. Fidelity. At the time the escapades of these fearless soldiers, their 'mad' Commander, Jack Langlais and Miss Madeleine Barclay were a mystery to all who lived in Chale, and probably still are to many, even though an account of their time in Chale in 1942 is to be found in two publications, including Fidelity Will Haunt Me Till I Die, by Peter Kingswell. And, a memorial to those who perished in 1942 can now be found in Chale Church.

Langlais, described as a Corsican, had adopted the name as a disguise; Mademoiselle Barclay, had adopted that name because it was where she banked. The other principal was Surgeon Lieutenant James Robertson who became well known locally and was the Medical Officer, and whose wife Mary later returned to be the Chale District Nurse after her husband had perished.

The Terrace, and the cliffs around Blackgang became their base and training area, and locals were astonished at the extra-ordinary training antics of the Commandos. Officers were living in private homes around the area. The garden of Inglestone was the base where a tented camp was established, and adjoining Lowcliffe Cottage which was to become their HQ, and its large garage the sick bay. Langlais and Barclay had bought and set up home in Arthur Wheeler's bungalow at the cliff edge, very near to Uffa Fox's cottage, although the relationship of an unmarried couple living together no doubt raised some eyebrows locally. Uffa greatly enjoyed the company of the Mad Commander.

On arrival in Chale, Robertson soon made his acquaintance with The Clarendon Hotel, where he was offered two rooms for his wife and himself and their young baby for just 28/- a week. The Roberts were playing their role. Langlais gave his permission for the family to come to The Clarendon. However, shortly after they were offered free accommodation in The Old Beacon, another house in The Terrace.

Training involved scaling and descending by ropes down the high cliffs at Blackgang, to the utter amazement of locals. Landing on the shore below the Chine also took place, albeit it was somewhat dangerous at times, to say the least.

There was no doubt an element of boredom amongst the Commandos, and they were not averse to helping themselves to a local supply of livestock, often having killed, cooked, and consumed the carcass before the unsuspecting farmer knew what had disappeared. One soldier used the Church clock as target practice, successfully hitting the dial from a good distance.

The arrival of a coloured French sailor in the Summer of 1942 by name of Daladier was an astonishment to the local boys who had never seen a black man in Chale before. The local policeman, PC Sampson, had lectured the school boys on the risks of talking too much to strangers in wartime, and the boys remembered this. They met the Frenchman on his bicycle outside The Clarendon Hotel, and their School. When he eventually made a request for directions to where the other Commandos were stationed, they carefully sent him off in the wrong direction before disappearing as quick as they could. He was very late for his appointment, but the rules of warfare were carried out by the local boys.

After months of severe training, the purpose was revealed. They were to go and fight the Japanese in Burma, on HMS Fidelity, the ship which Langlais had been given for the task. It was to be equipped with two seaplanes (which could be lowered into the water from the vessel). The project was greeted with some trepidation by the Officers, who considered the vague plans foolhardy to say the least, but Langlais was a determined man, and he drank a toast with his men with the words - *"To destiny, my friends. To death, and glory!"* Little did he know, or perhaps he did, that that was exactly what would happen.

The number of Marines was increased to nearly sixty, and they moved into larger houses along The Terrace. Fitness training was increased and steps were built from the end of the Terrace to the shore. Madeleine Barclay took an active part in the training, often firing a rifle over the heads of the men to 'encourage them'. On one occasion they took an old fishing boat from near the shore, which was unseaworthy. Seeing them, and unable to attract their attention by calling to them to turn round, she effected her command by firing her rifle at them; they turned and reached the shore just before the vessel was about to sink.

By reputation Barclay, an attractive 30 year old, had also used her undoubted female charms to 'encourage' some of the Officers, but their fear of Langlais should he find out, had brought a rejection of her affections (or so they said).

As the Summer of 1942 drew on, the training became less intense, particularly when Langlais was away making arrangements for the forthcoming voyage, and the Commandos spent more time in the comfort of local homes, or in the bar of The Clarendon Hotel. They even helped the school teacher establish and run a youth club in the school. The Commandos became popular with local residents, but still their reason for being in Chale was a mystery.

With Fidelity having been specially adapted and fitted out at Langlais' instructions for his invasion of Burma and the defeat of the Japs, by the end of October 1942 all the men had departed the village. In the December they set off, with Madelaine Barclay sailing with them with the rank of 1st Officer WRNS, believed to have been perhaps the only female to sail into action in the War. Was she a Spy or an Agent. Whatever, she was a remarkable, fearless character the like of which Chale had never seen before, or since!

The story of the fatal end of the Fidelity is taken from an account written by Octavia Roberts and sent to young Edward as read by her in the national press. Chale learned that it had been playing a significant role in the War.

"In December 1942, H.M.S. Fidelity was on her way to join the Eastern Fleet after having been specially fitted out. She carried two aircraft, a motor boat, and some landing craft. She joined a convoy which was sailing for Freetown, in Sierra Leone. In the vicinity of the Azores, early on December 27th, the convoy suffered an extremely heavy attack from German submarines. Several vessels were sunk so that the rescue vessel could not accommodate any more survivors. HMS Fidelity was therefore appointed rescue vessel that evening.

The attack continued throughout December 28th, and that afternoon in spite of the fact that the sea was very rough, the senior officer of escort asked Fidelity to send up one of her aircraft to assist in the defence of the convoy. Due to the roughness of the sea the attempt was unsuccessful; the plane crashed; and the crew rescued by one of the escorting destroyers. Later in the day several more ships were sunk, including that of the Vice-Admiral, W. Egerton.

Fidelity had developed some engine defect which was an after effect of damage sustained from the aircraft when it crashed, which had delayed her. One of the convoy stood escort by the stricken vessel, until early on 29th December she had to rejoin the convoy, when a tug was ordered from Gibraltar to go to HMS Fidelity's assistance. Progress was slow, but some repairs to her engines were effected enabling her to report that she was proceeding for the Azores.

In the afternoon, the second aircraft was flown off for reconnaissance, and was hoisted on board on her return, to take off again later. In the afternoon she reported having sighted two German submarines and started to engage them. The motor boat had already been lowered into the water to assist with hunting submarines. Shortly after a U-boat was again seen, and the motor boat tried to attack her with two landing craft, but without results. Shortly before 8pm she rescued the Commodore of the Convoy with some of the crew of his ship.

Shortly after midnight, on 30th December 1942, the motor boat began to report that she had lost sight of the Fidelity, but retained contact by radio telephony. The motor boat finally lost touch with her about 9.30 am, and was afterwards picked up by a destroyer".

Nothing further was ever heard of HMS Fidelity. On December 30th a force of destroyers was sent out to search for survivors, and this search continued until 7th January 1943, but no survivors were found. The Admiralty concluded that she was lost during the night of 31st December 1942/1st January 1943. There were claims that some may have survived, but with the crew of the aircraft, and the crew of the motor boat being rescued, this may have been the reason for these claims. There were also claims that some may have been taken prisoner by German submarines, which was given some credence by reports from German naval prisoners-of-war. It has been said that when the aircraft returned to the area where the Fidelity was last known to be, the weather was foggy, and no trace of her could be found. No survivors were ever found, and the mystery remains of the end of our visitors to Chale in 1942.

Two members of Chale Home Guard killed

An accident happened in the Chale Home Guard hut, which was located in the orchard behind Long Thatch, and Springfield, in Town Lane, Chale on 1st February 1944 which was to have a sickening affect on the whole community for some time to come. Henry Roberts, as will be seen elsewhere, did not join the Home Guard as he served as an Air Raid Warden; and Edward Roberts did not join as he was too young, and as an agricultural worker, in an exempt occupation. He joined up in the Army when he was still 18.

However, many men of the village who were not on active service, and others who had served during the Great War, joined the Chale Home Guard, and with younger Chale men formed the No 2 Platoon, 'E' Company, 19th Battalion Home Guard.

On the evening of 1st February the Company met for their usual training in the Hut. For this account of the incident, and to save any embarrassment to their families, I have purposely omitted to give the names of those involved, other than the hapless victims, as there was no blame attached to anyone involved, and verdicts of "Death by misadventure" was returned at the inquests on both men. The men were receiving instruction when a live round was fired inside the Hut. The bullet glanced off another piece of equipment in the hut and killed Private John Cheverton, aged 49, of Gladdices, Chale. It seriously wounded Private Philip Bullock, of Kingston, who sadly died a few days later in hospital.

At the inquest held in the Methodist School Room in Chale, it was stated that the Lieutenant who had given some instruction in the Hut had left to instruct others elsewhere. There were 19 men present, and Pte. Cheverton was cleaning a projector at one end of the hut, and others were being instructed on a Browning Machine Gun at the other end. Dummy ammunition was being used in the machine gun for training purposes, which was kept in a box. The box in question had been used many times before, and the dummy ammunition had wooden bullets which were painted red. They were much lighter in weight than live ammunition. However, after use the red paint wore off and the difference in appearance became less obvious. These dummies were always put back in the same box specially kept for them. No live ammunition was kept in the hut, and the men did not have live ammunition with them on such drills. Each man who had a rifle had ammunition at home.

The Coroner questioned "*Supposing someone did carry live ammunition to that drill?*". *The witness replied "It should not have happened".* The Coroner retorted *"It should not, but it did, apparently. It is amazing how such accidents happen. I have to enquire into them time after time, and I never seem to be able to get to the bottom of how live rounds get among blanks or dummies".* It was stated that the empty cartridge case found on the floor of the hut after the incident showed it to be the type used in machine guns. The ammunition in the possession of the men was different.

The witness said he could not suggest where a live round had come from. The hut was rather crowded. It was lit by two pressure paraffin lamps, and the light was good enough to read by. The difference in weight between live and dummy rounds was considerable, and would have been noticed. It was stated that it was impossible to get live ammunition from the stores without knowledge. All the men were aware that live ammunition should not be in the drill hut, and this was posted on the platoon notice board.

The Sergeant who was in charge of the machine gun and the ammunition, said he had used it the previous week; there were 10 rounds and he put them back in the box as usual. It was not kept locked. If there had been a live round in it he must have seen it. He was instructing on a Lewis Gun in another part of the hut when the live round was fired. He saw Pte Cheverton on the floor, and Pte Bullock walk away. They were both in front of the projector which was in line with the Browning machine gun.

The Coroner enquired if the hut was cleaned up periodically, and was told it was swept out the previous Sunday. It was stated that the bullet struck the projector and broke pieces of metal from it. The Coroner said what he wanted to know was how a live round could have got into the belt. No explanation could be given. He asked what would normally happen when preparing for a practice with the gun, and was told the dummies would be examined to make sure there were no live rounds there. *"Why would you do that?"*. *"To make sure there were no live rounds amongst them"*. *"Is there any chance of that happening"*. *"No, it would have been seen"*.

He asked *"Would a man picking up the ejected dummies from the floor put them in his pocket before refilling the belt?"* *" No, he would put them back in the belt as he picked them up. The men were not wearing ammunition pouches that night"*. It was explained that sometimes men might take them home in their pockets, and one might fall out of the clip into their pocket, and one might fall out of a pocket when picking up the dummies.

The Lance Corporal said that before the instruction commenced he put 10 rounds of dummies into the belt, from the box. He looked at each one as he put them in, and he was certain they were all dummies. Twice the belt was used, and twice the belt went through the gun before the live round was fired. *"Do you carry any ammunition in your pocket"* *" No, Sir. I use a Sten gun which has quite different ammunition"*.

The Private who fired the gun with the fatal round in it said he had rifle ammunition at home but he never took any to drills. They remained in his equipment pouches at home and he never put any in his pockets. When asked, he said he was quite sure he did not have a live round on him that night.

The Private who picked up the used dummies from the floor after the previous firing said he was not talking to anyone, and was not in a hurry. He doubted that he would have detected a live round by its extra weight, and he could not see very well as the other men in the hut cast shadows. He could not see well enough to notice the colour of the bullets. He was asked if he noticed anything unusual in the hut that evening, and whether the hut was overcrowded. He replied *"No, but the light was not good"*.

The doctor who examined the body said it had a deep wound in the left groin which had lacerated the femoral artery, and which would have caused death within a minute. The wound was not consistent with a simple bullet wound, but seemed to have been caused by fragments of steel consistent with the bullet having broken up when it hit the projector. The spent bullet could not be found.

In summing up the Coroner said the unfortunate accident remained a complete mystery, but it was a warning for anyone not to get in front of any lethal weapon. It seemed impossible that a live bullet could have got into the gun, but it did. No blame could be placed against anyone, and he appreciated the problems which members of the Home Guard often faced. However *familiarity breeds contempt, and you can get so used to your weapons that you think that nothing can go wrong, until one of these unfortunate accidents happen*. Sympathy was expressed to the family.

Several days later, the other victim, Pte Philip Bullock died of his stomach injuries sustained in the same incident. A second inquest was carried out by the same Coroner. It was revealed that death had occurred due to a gangrenous perforation of the bowel. A similar verdict of "Death by misadventure" was recorded.

Military funerals were held at Chale Church for Pte. Cheverton, and at Kingston Church for Pte. Bullock, and both graves are marked with Military gravestones.

Chale Home Guard and Scouts - Armistice Day Parade 1940

Henry Roberts, A.R.P. Warden - reporting for duty

CHAPTER 14

THE AIR RAID WARDEN, AND OTHER WARTIME SERVICES

Henry Roberts served with distinction in the Great War, and was well trained to carry that experience forward to the anticipated events which would surely present themselves should Nazi Germany attack Great Britain. Whilst the Second World War was not declared until 1939, and no real attempt to invade our shores was made until 1940, Chale was prepared long before that!

Henry Roberts was appointed an Air Raid Warden in July 1938. He was also appointed a member of the "Messenger Service" staff.

From the time of appointment as a Warden, Henry, like his fellow Wardens, were given training in various situations which might appear. Tom Sprake, Octavia's Cousin, was a Chief Air Raid Warden and involved in training, and no doubt had some influence in enrolling Henry. Henry attended lectures and courses, and amongst these he attended and passed his examination in Anti-Gas Training undertaken between 2nd November 1938 and 4th January 1939.

When War was eventually declared on 3rd September 1939, Chale was ready. The invasion was expected that afternoon, and an A.R.P. Hut was established next to the Post Office near the Church in Chale.

Protecting the A.R.P. Hut near Chale Church 1939

Within hours sand bags were prepared and stacked to protect the hut, by local men, and if the photograph is an indication, by boys as well. Everyone joined in. So impressive was the protection against the expected bombs that it was pictured in the County Press with the anonymous title "A well-protected first-aid point in an Island Village". No enemy invader could possibly know where it was, except that a rather distinctive view of Chale Church is clearly seen in the background!

Henry, and the other Wardens, were issued with their 'tin helmets' with the familiar "W" on the front and back; with arm bands declaring their title; and uniforms which resembled boiler-suits. Henry's 'Bag' contained his Gas Mask; bandages; whistle; and other items of warning; and Gas Protection Eyeshields. All of these survived almost intact for over sixty years in his home at Denhams, together with the metal sign - AIR RAID WARDEN- which would have been screwed onto his front door. In many villages, the Air Raid Warden would have operated from his own home.

LIGHTS BRING BOMBS!

"AN INTELLIGENCE officer whose job it is to question Nazi airman prisoners told me this one.

He asked an airman if he could explain why so many bombs were dropped on small villages—on lonely farms—by country roadsides and on sparsely populated areas where—as the Germans probably knew—there were no military objectives whatever.

The airman replied at once. He said "**We always drop a bomb where we can see a light.**"

Well—that's indiscriminate bombing all right—but, presuming that the A.A. barrage drives the raider away from his military objective—he is not going to zoom back to Germany with a full bomb rack. He's going to let fly somewhere.

A glint of light is almost certainly a building with people in it—but pitch darkness may be the middle of nothing.

So do take the black-out very seriously for the sake of your neighbours. And see that they take it seriously, too—for the sake of you and your family. It's a fact that a chink of ground light can be seen from a plane flying at a great height.

Don't let them catch a glimpse of you and yours ! "

Reproduced by permission of the " Daily Mirror" and Printed by James Heap (Hanley 1925) Ltd., Booth Street, Stoke-on-Trent

Many leaflets warning the public of the 'Invader' were issued from 1939. These are just a few.

If the INVADER comes

Issued by the Ministry of Information in co-operation with the War Office and the Ministry of Home Security.

WHAT TO DO — AND HOW TO DO IT

THE Germans threaten to invade Great Britain. If they do so they will be driven out by our Navy, our Army and our Air Force. Yet the ordinary men and women of the civilian population will also have their part to play. Hitler's invasions of Poland, Holland and Belgium were greatly helped by the fact that the civilian population was taken by surprise. They did not know what to do when the moment came. *You must not be taken by surprise.* This leaflet tells you what general line you should take. More detailed instructions will be given you when the danger comes nearer. Meanwhile, read these instructions carefully and be prepared to carry them out.

I

When Holland and Belgium were invaded, the civilian population fled from their homes. They crowded on the roads, in cars, in carts, on bicycles and on foot, and so helped the enemy by preventing their own armies from advancing against the invaders. You must not allow that to happen here. Your first rule, therefore, is :—

(1) IF THE GERMANS COME, BY PARACHUTE, AEROPLANE OR SHIP, YOU MUST REMAIN WHERE YOU ARE. THE ORDER IS "STAY PUT".

If the Commander in Chief decides that the place where you live must be evacuated, he will tell you when and how to leave. Until you receive such orders you must remain where you are. If you run away, you will be exposed to greater danger because you will be machine gunned from the air as were civilians in Holland and Belgium, and you will also block the roads by which our own armies will advance to turn the Germans out.

II

There is another method which the Germans adopt in their invasion. They make use of the civilian population in order to create confusion and panic. They spread false rumours and issue false instructions. In order to prevent this, you should obey the second rule, which is as follows :—

(2) DO NOT BELIEVE RUMOURS AND DO NOT SPREAD THEM. WHEN YOU RECEIVE AN ORDER, MAKE QUITE SURE THAT IT IS A TRUE ORDER AND NOT A FAKED ORDER. MOST OF YOU KNOW YOUR POLICEMEN AND YOUR A.R.P. WARDENS BY SIGHT, YOU CAN TRUST THEM. IF YOU KEEP YOUR HEADS, YOU CAN ALSO TELL WHETHER A MILITARY OFFICER IS REALLY BRITISH OR ONLY PRETENDING TO BE SO. IF IN DOUBT ASK THE POLICEMAN OR THE A.R.P. WARDEN. USE YOUR COMMON SENSE.

★ The place of farmers and farm workers is on duty every day and all day on the farm, producing every ounce of food they can, until other orders are received from the military or the police.

STICK TO YOUR FARM AND CARRY ON

ISSUED BY THE MINISTRY OF AGRICULTURE AND FISHERIES
(12709) Wt. 20746/P1352 200,000 7/41 K.H.K. Gp. 8

V

...a may be asked by Army and Air Force officers to help ...ny ways. For instance, the time may come when you ...receive orders to block roads or streets in order to prevent ...enemy from advancing. Never block a road unless you ...ld which one you must block. Then you can help by ...g trees, wiring them together or blocking the roads with ... Here, therefore, is the fifth rule :—

5) BE READY TO HELP THE MILITARY IN ANY WAY. BUT DO NOT BLOCK ROADS UNTIL ORDERED TO DO SO BY THE MILITARY OR L.D.V. AUTHORITIES.

VI

...you are in charge of a factory, store or other works, ...ise its defence at once. If you are a worker, make sure ...you understand the system of defence that has been ...ised and know what part you have to play in it. ...mber always that parachutists and fifth column men are

...must know in advance who is to take command, who ...e second in command, and how orders are to be ...itted. This chain of command must be built up a...ll probably find that ex-officers or N.C.O.'s, who ... emergencies before, are the best people to underta... ...ommand. The sixth rule is therefore as follows :—

) IN FACTORIES AND SHOPS, ALL MANAGERS AND MEN AND WORKMEN SHOULD ORGANISE SOME SYSTEM NOW BY WHICH A SUDDEN ATTACK CAN BE RESISTED.

Farmers!

WHAT TO DO IF THE INVADER COMES

★ The general public has been told "should the invader come, stand firm." On farms the first duty of farmers and farm workers is to go on producing all the food possible.

This means that, unless military action in the immediate neighbourhood makes it impossible, farmers and farm workers must go on ploughing, cultivating, sowing, hoeing and harvesting as though no invasion were occurring. Some of our Kentish people have worked unperturbed in their fields with shells screaming over their heads. So can we all—and we must.

★ You need your tractors and other motor driven vehicles to carry on with your job. But such vehicles would also be very useful to the enemy if he could capture them; tractors would be especially useful to him in coastal areas where landings may be attempted.

It is, therefore, your duty to put your vehicles out of action if they are in danger of capture by the enemy. You will probably receive orders from the police, A.R.P. wardens, or the military; but, whether you do so or not, you should in any case disable your vehicles when there is an obvious risk of their being captured.

To put your vehicles out of action, remove the distributor head and leads, and either empty the tank or remove the carburettor; in the case of diesel engines, remove the injection pump and connection. The parts removed must be hidden well away from the vehicle.

In the 'bag' was an envelope marked "EYESHIELDS, Anti-Gas, Mk.11. - with the following instructions printed thereon:-

AIR SPRAY

IMMEDIATE ACTION to be taken to prevent blisters

1.	COTTON WASTE	Swab liquid off exposed skin.
2.	OINTMENT	Rub vigorously on exposed skin for ½ minute, using both hands.
3.	EYESHIELD	If detector shows large drops, remove garment away as necessary. Rub OINTMENT on skin now exposed. If cape worn, swab off liquid.
4.	DETECTORS and WEAPONS	Remove and renew detectors - Decontaminate weapons.
5.	OINTMENT	Re-apply to hands rubbing hard for ½ minute.

The transparent plastic type eyeshields do not look as if they would have offered much protection, but were better than nothing, and no doubt all that was available at the time. A compound contained in a tube bears the wording:-

OUTFIT ANTI-DIMMING Mk 2

Instructions for use

Clean the eyepiece with the cloth provided.
Breathe on the eyepiece and apply a little
compound evenly with the finger.
Breathe on the eyepiece again and polish
VERY lightly with the cloth so that a thin
layer of the compound remains.

A small roll of 'Medium Mines Dressing' in a sealed paper packet bears the wording:

Directions -

Wrap the dressing round the wound.
Avoid touching the pad.

Perhaps thankfully they survive because they were never needed, and never used.

The general establishment for Chale was that it came under the control of Ventnor, with the local Head Warden being Tom Sprake. Henry Roberts Post was No. 13, and it had its own telephone - number Niton 286. The Post covered the area from Chale Church, Chale Farm, King Hall to the Wesleyan Chapel on the corner of Newman Lane.

The compliment of the Chale Wardens was made up of Tom Sprake (Senior Warden); Bruce Dabell (Second Warden); and Other Wardens - J. Harris (Post Office); W. Sprake (Church Place); F. Mew (Sunnyside); T. Brown (Shop); J. Merwood (Bellevista); R. Merwood (Beamans); R. Barton (Church Place); G. Hardy (Newman Lane); and Henry Roberts (Denhams). The Wardens Handbook includes the following signals - Caution, Yellow; Action Raid, Red; Raiders passed, green; Cancelled or All-Clear, white.

Numerous handbooks and instruction leaflets were issued, many relating to protection against a Gas Attack. One poignantly bears the statement

HITLER WILL SEND NO WARNING. practice putting on your Gas Mask.

The Air Rid Warden was responsible for establishing numbers of Gas Masks needed, and for distributing them. There were three sizes, Large, Medium, and Small, and those for babies. Henry's distribution was 15 large; 26 medium, and 4 small, an indication of how small the village population was at that time.

Whilst Henry Roberts continued to keep his diaries all through the War years, there are only the following entries, all in 1940, which refer to the A.R.P. and air raids on Chale:-

2nd June - *A.R.P. practice this afternoon. Wardens out, and First Aid parties. Yellow signal (Action, Raid) came through just before 8 o'clock tonight for real raid. Will Sprake called me. He, Tim Harris, Ray Barton, and myself stayed up Post Office hut until 3.30am (Monday). Police car from Ventnor came and said a plane fired at the search light on Ventnor Pier with tracer bullets. Reported brought down on Ashey Down, also one of our planes.*

17th June - *Two bombs dropped by Germans up on Down, just missed road and water main, and some heifers lower side of road. Wardens fetched out until about 4.00am.*

24th June - *Called out for air raid 12.15 until 3.30am*
25th June - *Called out for air raid 12 until 3 o'clock*
26th June - *Called out for air raid 11.30pm to 3 am*

10th October - *Sale at 'Halls', Chale Green. There were three air raid warnings while the sale was on.*

....

Amongst the records found were the following reports written on ARP/MI forms - 'Warden's Report Form'. Unfortunately these are not dated and I cannot find any local knowledge of the incidents.

One report appears to relate to the sighting of Paratroops landing at Atherfield Holiday Camp, about two miles from Chale, proceeded by dive bombing, as reported by the local Home Guard. Another report refers to an occurrence 'In sea about ½ mile out off Chale'. A third report refers to 3 casualties outside Chale Schools Shelter, with others trapped inside. (An air raid shelter with a school room inside was built in the grounds of Chale School, where the school playing field is now, for use of the children in the event of a raid. My understanding is that it was only ever used once or twice as it was very damp!).

In a letter written to Edward on 30th January 1944, Henry Roberts says *"We had an alarm up Hut from 9 - 11 pm; and another from 3.45 am to 5.50 am this morning"*. The times do not exactly match, but could this be one of these incidents, or was it just a training exercise?

Warden Report Forms - was this nearly the invasion of England?

....

In 1938, the Home Office Air Raid Precautions Department issued a leaflet on making Garden Trench Shelters for six people. This involved initially digging a trench 2ft deep, 4ft wide, and 10ft long (which the pamphlet stated would take one man 4 hours to dig), which would provide protection for 6 people, lying down. Subsequent enlargement (presumably if you had survived) involved lowering the trench to a depth of 4ft 6ins, making it generally bigger, with wooden supports, and a corrugated tin roof. Dug earth formed a bank on each side, and sand bags or earth filled soap boxes provided further support. Eventually the roof was covered with earth and turfs to hide its existence. A ladder at one end provided access, and an entrance was protected by a gas curtain consisting of a blanket with wooden slats fixed every foot to keep it hanging, and trailing onto the ground. This blanket had to be kept wet to keep out the gas.

Subsequent improvements could involve benches to sit or sleep on, and means of storage for food and reading material, and possibly a wireless. The ground was to be sloping to one end to drain any water which would enter the shelter. Further boarding or corrugated sheets were to prevent the walls falling in. To avoid damage from falling masonry, the shelter was recommended to be built at least 20ft from a building.

One such shelter was built along the road in Town Lane, Chale, by Percy Sprake, conveniently dug into the roadside bank where a stone wall existed through which the entrance was made at road level allowing any water to drain away. Substantial scrap metal supports were used instead of timber, and the whole thing was apparently built to a high standard and fitted out with some spare furniture and a bed for comfort. It was used once overnight as a trial, but did not prove very comfortable! One fact was omitted from the pamphlet - the effect of animals! Cows were allowed to graze in the field where the shelter was dug, and shortly after its construction, they took to walking over the earth mound. Their weight forced the roof to collapse, and the whole structure fell in. It was never reconstructed, and luckily was never needed.

....

Another important establishment was the Red Cross & St John C.H.S.S. (Central Hospital Supply Service) Depot in Chale. This was run by Miss Wallis and Miss Aubrey from No.1 The Terrace.

In a letter to Edward then stationed at Elgin in Scotland, on 31st December 1943, in which she enclosed a miniature Letts Diary for 1944, Miss Wallis writes:-

"Thank you so much for your kind Christmas Wishes. We were both so pleased to hear from you, and to know from your people that you are getting on so well. We send you a small Diary with our best wishes for the New Year.

Perhaps you have acquired a repertoire of old Scottish songs! If so, you will have to sing them at Chale Socials after the War! So I give you warning!

Chale is much as usual. The influenza germ has been busy. Miss Aubrey and I have been terrifically busy right up to Christmas Eve making and selling toys in aid of the Red Cross, and we hope with the aid of the Chale Service Cadets to send in a cheque for about £50. It is so astonishing how these things sell round about Christmas! Saunders Roe of Cowes (the War-workers) asked us to make over 200 toys for sale for the Red X, but of course we have now practically no workers who can attend the Depot, although lots of knitting is still done outside."

One local resident, Mrs Emily Woodford, who lived in part of Denhams Cottage, knitted over 50 garments for the C.H.S.S. Depot during the war years. As has been recorded earlier, War Savings, and the Wings for Victory fundraising in Chale alone had raised nearly £12,000 by 1943, and more later.

Chale worked hard to support the War effort.

ORDER OF THE DAY

To members of the Civil Defence (General) Services.

The tide of war has at last receded from the homes of the people and the time is come when Civil Defence (General) Services are being demobilised.

At this moment I wish to express to local authorities and their Officers, to the men and women of those Services, and to all those who have shared as helpers in the post-raid organisations including members of the W.V.S., my deep gratitude for what they have done in the long years of war.

In the time of heaviest attack there were nearly two hundred thousand whole-time members of the Services and one million and a quarter part-time members. There are now only some thirty-five thousand whole-time members and considerably less than a million part-time members; and I do not forget in this expression of gratitude those who have already left the Services.

Before the first great attack fell on London in September, 1940, no man could say how the Civil Defence organisations would work or how the Services would respond to the calls upon them. Once the attack started the issue was never in doubt.

The local authorities and their officers did their share magnificently and local government justified to the full the confidence that had been placed in it. Of the members of the Services we must all speak with honour and high praise.

Whether it be the Wardens, or the Rescue Parties, the Ambulance and First Aid Post Services or those in the Report Centres, you all showed through those long nights and days of watchfulness, danger and toil, a loyalty to your Services, a devotion to those in suffering and peril, and an unfailing courage which have brought to your uniform an honour that takes rank with the historic emblems of British greatness.

Your Services are no longer required for active Civil Defence: but the Country will have need of your spirit of comradeship and service in the difficult days ahead. Too much leisure has been taken from you during the war, it is a precious part of home and family life; but I hope you may be able to spare some of it for the neighbourly tasks of the community in which you live.

You will take with you many memories of which you will have a right to be very proud, but none of you will have a prouder or happier memory than I in being associated with you in this great task so well accomplished.

To each one of you I give my thanks as I bid you farewell and Godspeed.

My colleagues the Secretary of State for Scotland and the Minister of Health, who have been associated with me in administration of the Services are in the fullest accord with this message and have asked me to convey to you their thanks and good wishes.

HERBERT MORRISON.

Ministry of Home Security,
2nd May, 1945.

W. BLAKE AND SON, PRINTERS 4, TOWN LANE, NEWPORT.

The War is over!

CHAPTER 15

OFF TO GET THE 'JERRYS', AND GET HOME AGAIN

With the pending liberation of Europe by the combined British Commonwealth and American troops, known as the Allied Expeditionary Force under the command of General Dwight D. Eisenhower, it may not be surprising that few letters were kept either by soldier Edward Roberts or his parents in Chale. The risk of vital information being revealed to an invading enemy was still a great threat and meant that anything which might help them should not be kept. Having completed his initial training, and now well equipped to be a driver in the British Army, Edward was eventually dispatched to form part of the D-Day force. Not, luckily, to be in the first wave of troops to cross the Channel, almost in sight of his Chale home, but to follow a few days later once a foothold had been established on French soil. It is understood Edward went on D-Day+4.

HEADQUARTERS SECOND ARMY
ISSUE OF SPECIAL ITEMS

1. Certain items of special rations and equipment are being issued by the Camp Commandant to all personnel prior to embarkation.

2. There is a reason for the issue of each separate item. These reasons are given below so that all offrs and other ranks are aware of the importance of the issue.

3. The items are NOT replaceable, and care must be taken against loss.

4. Any personnel found to have consumed any item of the issue before the appointed time will be liable to severe disciplinary action.

24 Hour Ration Packs

All personnel are issued with two 24 hr ration packs with the exception of those landing on D Day who are issued with one 24 hr Ration Pack (Type 'A' and one 24 hr ration pack (not type 'A').

These, together with a Tommy Cooker and a water sterilizing outfit are for the first 48 hrs of landing. They must not be consumed before landing, as no other rations will be available.

EMERGENCY RATION

Not to be consumed under any circumstances unless no other form of subsistence is available and then only upon orders of an offr.

PRESERVED MEAT

One tin is issued to all personnel landing up to and including D + 2, to supplement the two 24 hr ration packs.

CHEWING GUM

Personnel landing on D Day, get a packet of Chewing Gum each to alleviate sea-sickness during the voyage.

BISCUITS AND CHOCOLATE

All offrs and ORs are issued with a packet of biscuits and two bars of chocolate. These are for consumption during the period between leaving for embarkation and actually arriving on board.

MATCHES

No matches are available for issue. All ranks are advised to obtain at least one box of matches under private arrangements and to carry them wrapped in some waterproof material.

BAGS, VOMIT

Issued on the scale of three per officer and other rank.

'Q' Branch
1 Jun 44   10 mds/146

A leaflet issued to soldiers prior to D-Day 1944
(This travelled to France, and all over Europe!)

Words of encouragement for the tasks ahead from Eisenhower were relayed by a printed message, ending with "Good Luck! And let us all beseech the blessing of Almighty God upon this great and noble undertaking." This, and the instruction leaflet about special rations etc. for the journey need no further comment, except to say that they were kept secure on the resultant journey which took Edward across northern France; through Holland; and into Germany itself. He had achieved what his father never had - he reached Berlin.

Driving a motor vehicle was perhaps not Edward's first choice; indeed it is probably true to say that he never really got the hang of it, but the need to transport men, supplies, and ammunition to the front line, and then return with men, and later prisoners, was a task ahead for Edward to achieve, and he did.

As the expeditionary forces proceeded relentlessly across Europe, other risks faced the troops. Britain had been at war with Germany ever since 1914; peace had never been declared after the Great War. Indeed some British troops from the earlier conflict had remained in Germany and had married into or become part of German families. This situation posed a potential risk, and in several leaflets from the Commander-in-Chied, Field Marshal Montgomery - "Monty" to his troops, on Non-Fraternisation, the risks were spelled out of associating with local people in occupied Countries. But there was also the need to treat local residents with respect, unlike the enemy did when they

**SUPREME HEADQUARTERS
ALLIED EXPEDITIONARY FORCE**

Soldiers, Sailors and Airmen of the Allied Expeditionary Force!

You are about to embark upon the Great Crusade, toward which we have striven these many months. The eyes of the world are upon you. The hopes and prayers of liberty-loving people everywhere march with you. In company with our brave Allies and brothers-in-arms on other Fronts, you will bring about the destruction of the German war machine, the elimination of Nazi tyranny over the oppressed peoples of Europe, and security for ourselves in a free world.

Your task will not be an easy one. Your enemy is well trained, well equipped and battle-hardened. He will fight savagely.

But this is the year 1944! Much has happened since the Nazi triumphs of 1940-41. The United Nations have inflicted upon the Germans great defeats, in open battle, man-to-man. Our air offensive has seriously reduced their strength in the air and their capacity to wage war on the ground. Our Home Fronts have given us an overwhelming superiority in weapons and munitions of war, and placed at our disposal great reserves of trained fighting men. The tide has turned! The free men of the world are marching together to Victory!

I have full confidence in your courage, devotion to duty and skill in battle. We will accept nothing less than full Victory!

Good Luck! And let us all beseech the blessing of Almighty God upon this great and noble undertaking.

Dwight D Eisenhower

Eisenhower's message to the Allied Expeditionary Force prior to D-Day.

invaded these Countries. In March 1945 he concluded in one message - "Be just; be firm; be correct, and don't argue. Last time we won the war and let the peace slip out of our hands. This time we must win both the war, and the peace". By July 1945 the instructions were eased a little, allowing soldiers to engage in conversation with adult Germans in the streets and in public places.

Edward admitted that driving was not a task he relished! Speed with a motor was of little interest for someone brought up by the steady pace of a horse. By all accounts he did not like the risk of going round a corner, so would stop and engage first gear before making the manoeuvre around each obstacle. On one occasion in his journey across Europe his vehicle broke down, and he was left by the roadside for some 48 hours until a mechanic could attend to his vehicle. Edward used the time to read, eat, and 'have a rest'. Many convoys passed him on their way to and from the front line; but Edward remained alone. There was a little scare when a German plane flew over firing at the ground, just missing him, but he took that in his stride!

On reaching Brussels he was issued with a leaflet setting out the correct way for soldiers to conduct themselves, including where entertainment could be found. Of note is the Montgomery Club, and Café Blighty; new names for no-doubt older establishments!

On reaching Germany, there was an opportunity to take 'souvenirs' and

SUPREME HEADQUARTERS
ALLIED EXPEDITIONARY FORCE

TO ALL MEMBERS OF THE ALLIED EXPEDITIONARY FORCE:

The task which we set ourselves is finished, and the time has come for me to relinquish Combined Command.

In the name of the United States and the British Commonwealth, from whom my authority is derived, I should like to convey to you the gratitude and admiration of our two nations for the manner in which you have responded to every demand that has been made upon you. At times, conditions have been hard and the tasks to be performed arduous. No praise is too high for the manner in which you have surmounted every obstacle.

I should like, also, to add my own personal word of thanks to each one of you for the part you have played, and the contribution you have made to our joint victory.

Now that you are about to pass to other spheres of activity, I say Good-bye to you and wish you Good Luck and God-Speed.

Dwight Eisenhower

Eisenhower's message when the War was won

Edward took possession of two Nazi Iron Crosses, and possibly other items, which he retained all his life.

There were several opportunities for leave, and each time he returned for a short sojourn, it enabled him to take up farming tasks at home in Chale, helping his father. In a letter sent in March 1945 there was a comment that he *"Got the boat from Dover and crossed to France. We had a French train and the seats were very uncomfortable"*!

By March 1946, with the return from Europe, Edward may have wished for a discharge on grounds of his work in agriculture, but all requests were rejected. The Army needed drivers in Egypt. On 13th March 1946 he wrote home - *We set sail tomorrow. We have 5,000 Italians below going home, and 2000 troops on board.*

1946

15th March - An aunt to Edward. *We had a Conservative meeting in Clarendon on Thursday. It is different in there* (under new management now) *not much furniture and no carpet, but a nice fire and very warm!*

16th March - Edward to Mam. *We should be in Gib tomorrow. I have been on Guard Duty. The Italians are a scruffy lot and bad sailors; a few of our boys have 'shot the cat', but I'm alright and hungry as a hunter. We get fresh bread every day, it is very good, I could eat a loaf at a time. Cigarettes are 6d. for 20!*

19th March - Edward to Mam. *When we got to Gib the boat was surrounded by bum-boats selling watches, silk stockings, and Cognac. The Captain ordered the hoses to be turned on them to stop the crew getting any booze, but some managed to get some - £1 for 3 bottles! We had a sweepstake on the daily run, and I won 2/6 for guessing 310 miles; if I had said 311 I would have won ten bob!*

27th March - Mam to Edward. *Hope you are enjoying the trip and having the time of your life what with new bread every day. I suppose you don't get onions thrown in as well? If you did you would never finish eating and get so fat you won't be able to see out!*

28th March - Edward to Mam. *I'm glad Dad has got a new collar for Dandy, and that you have got the pram wheels back* (for the milk trolley)

18th April - Mam to Edward. *Dad has been ploughing up a bit of garden up 'Saeter'. He sent off Minnie's cow calf on Tuesday, a week old, and he got £3.50, a good price. We have got plenty of milk now, which pleases the customers, and we will need it for Easter. Dad went to see if he could get you out* (of the army) *on the Class 'B' scheme; he has to write to the Ministry of Food.*

22nd April - Mam to Edward. *Dad went to a sale and bought a weighing bucket and two bottle frames to go in the sterilizer tank for putting the milk bottles in; it is easier than putting them in rows on top of each other. When Dad went in to milk this afternoon 5 cows were missing, so he milked the ones that were there for me to have enough milk to go round, then went and looked for them. They had gone up the New Road; he has had two days this week that they have served him that trick, so he has got another electric fencer for round here!*

29th April - Mam to Edward. *Dad's been to two meetings; one in Newport on heat treatment of all milk, the other down Star was a Growmore meeting. I sent you a parcel with 3 tins of boot polish; 2oz tobacco; and a tablet of toilet soap, all I could get. I hope it will be alright for your skin.*

12th May - Mam to Edward. *I am writing this while I am listening to the Service on the wireless. They have just sung the hymn for absent ones - 'Holy Father in thy mercy, hear our anxious prayer'. Now F. Marshal Montgomery is speaking for the Soldiers Benevolent Fund. Well, now I must get on with my letter.*

You remember I told you the Oats down Cricket Field did not grow. Well, they came out with an International Crawler Tractor and a three furrow plough at 11 o'clock on Thursday and finished ploughing on Friday; then went through three times with the cultivator, and on Monday Fisk & Fisher are sending out 25cwt fertilizer, and Farmers Trading (now SCATS) are sending out 25cwt Magestic Potatoes, and they hope to get them in by Wednesday. Cricket Field will have a good Spring Clean as they have got to be harrowed three times, then hoed and baulked up. I hope there will be some pay attached to the end of it!

16th May - Mam to Edward. *Well we have got the spuds in down Cricket Field. Seven or eight Jerry prisoners came yesterday to put them in; they were about 5½ hours doing the job, I hope they will come up alright. There was 10 cwt more left than they wanted so Dad is going to put them in down Welshes. Dad sold the five heifers to Harold Biles the other week; they were such a nuisance getting out, so now he has got rid of them. We hope you will be home by hay making time.*

20th May - Edward to Mam. *We have arrived in Egypt. I was in Alex for the first time, but the evening was spoiled by the Wags starting a riot. We did not get into trouble, but two of our boys are in hospital due to some well aimed bricks going through their windscreen. I hope the spuds will come up alright down Cricket Field. I see from the paper that the Debating Society meets up Clarendon.*

4th June - Mam to Edward. *They are going to have a Victory Parade in London on Saturday. They have decided not to have any tea or anything here owing to the food shortage. They are arranging a party to go round the Island but you have to put your name down for that at the Post Office. They are going to have a United Service next Sunday. We can now get a bus from Blackgang to Sandown, and there is one that runs from Blackgang to Yarmouth on Sundays, so that makes a nice trip, and they may run it on Saturdays too, soon.*

9th June - Mam to Edward. *They had the Victory Celebrations in London, but the weather was bad. We put up two flags; one on the gate and one on the dairy door, but there were not many more around here. We have just heard on the wireless that Montgomery has flown to Egypt, so you might see him. I have been painting round our room.*

26th June - Mabel to Edward. *I am sending you 2oz Battleaxe; hope you like it. Dad has had the blacksmith out to shoe Dandy. He had him in the disc-harrow down Welshes and he managed very well. George is in a funk, one hand short - Frank Urry was taken to hospital with pneumonia and isn't getting on fast. I know it is a nuisance, but one can't help getting ill! I caught two rabbits in the garden; one in a wire and one in a gin. We have been plagued with young rabbits and they have eaten everything in the garden, so I thought I would have a go at catching them. Have you heard on the wireless that a convict has escaped and has been seen nearly all over the Island; he was said to have paid Chale a visit.*

5th July - Mam to Edward. *We have just started picking Loganberries; we have sold several pounds of Gooseberries. Dad and Mabel have just come in from hay carting. We won't be having Mr Downie to help any more as he died yesterday. We have just heard that Bread, Flour, and Cakes are going to be rationed from 21st July. I have got my spectacles back so I will be able to see better to write now.*

(Every letter referred to asking when Edward could get out of the Army, but no such luck)

7th July - Edward to Mam. *I'm glad they caught the convict that was loose; it would have been a bad mark for the Island if he had got away! I hope the weather will be alright for hay making.*

2nd August - Mam to Edward. *I hope you won't be going to Palestine, there are funny things going on there with the Jews.* (What changes!). *We had the Show (Chale Show) yesterday, and it was a lovely day. We did not go down, but the Town Lane people all went up; it was a good show by all accounts, and a lot of people there.*

No further letters, but on 25th August 1946 Edward Roberts was Released to the Reserve on grounds of National Importance - Class "B" releases, to enable him to 'return to work of national importance' - farm work. A hand written note stated of "*T/14510943 Dvr. Roberts T. - A hard and willing worker, clean, and has performed his duties with zeal and ability*". Within weeks he was back home in Chale. The journey home took him back through the Mediterranean and by rail across France to Dieppe, (from where his father had travelled back to home in 1919). His service as a soldier over, for good!

Just one final appointment. On 18th October 1946 Edward was unanimously elected to the British Legion, Chale Branch and advised of this by the Rev. C. Sinclair, branch Secretary. He had to pay half a crown (2/6d) (or 12 ½ p) for the honour. His badge was to be presented to him at the forthcoming Dinner, to which he was entitled to bring one girlfriend, free of charge. He never did get a girlfriend, whether free of charge, or not!, and remained a bachelor all his life.

On return home, Edward was soon working on his father's farm at Denhams. But for him life had changed for ever. When he left for Army service, The Clarendon was still in his families hands and his grand-father, Tom Roberts was still alive. Now both had gone.

The following years saw Edward helping and eventually taking on many roles in the village of Chale with his father. He became the local grave-digger which he did for many years. They would receive a card from the local Undertaker with the exact measurements of each coffin, from which they dug the grave, just 1 inch larger than the measurements shown. These were always the external measurements of the coffin, but on one occasion, the internal measurement was given, and the coffin almost got stuck - as Edward once said, "it scraped both sides as it went down!" He was eventually appointed as Sexton and Verger at Chale Church.

Edward Roberts - Sexton at
St. Andrew's Church, Chale

He became a School Manager at Chale School where his great-aunt Martha Brown had been the Infants teacher. He became a member of the Blackgang Auxiliary Rescue service, which he served for forty years, becoming Auxiliary in Charge, and received the 25 years and 40 years service medal and bar. He was a member of Chale Parochial Church Council; a member of Chale Horticultural Society where he helped run the sports for many years at the annual show; and a supporter and member of many other village activities.

Having been a young Boy Scout before the War, he passed on the skills he had learned to others and

Edward Roberts - Verger at St. Andrew's Church, Chale

was an Assistant Scout Master in Chale for many years. He was skilled at 'knots', and much time was taken demonstrating how to make various knots, but he was often so quick at doing them that his pupils could not easily learn his skills - but they all enjoyed his company!

But farming was never his forte! He worked on the farm until his father's death in 1961, and was often seen delivering milk. He had a small car, which he never really enjoyed driving! This sometimes became the butt of fun for local boys, who, on one occasion at least, during a spell of cold weather and with a sheet of ice on a steep part of the roadway, called out to Edward that his rear wheel was going round. On hearing this he stopped the car to inspect the problem, only to be greeted with laughter and quickly disappearing boys. On attempting to move off again, the ice proved impossible, and with no-one to help, he was stuck until help came along. On another occasion, when the vehicle broke down, it was seen being towed home, with Edward at the wheel, by a horse!

But it was 'Up Clarendon' where he liked to spend his time, in his favourite corner, where locals and visitors alike wanting to hear a good 'yarn' would ply him with rum, and he would oblige!

And this is the image many will recall of Edward Roberts.

Edward Roberts in his favourite chair
in The Clarendon Bar

On his death in 2004, Edward left a treasure of village memorabilia and family records which he and his family had kept safe and sound for over 150 years, and from which this book has been prepared. A unique record, and a unique tribute to a unique family, and to a unique village. His grandfather was described as 'the grand old man of Chale'. Indeed, all the Roberts family are justly described as - grand 'Men of Chale'.

Edward Roberts - in retirement

CHAPTER 16

MORE DIARIES - 1948 TO 1953

During this period Henry Roberts continued to keep a diary, but only those of 1948, 1949, 1952, and 1953 survive. These final records provide us with further evidence of how life was changing forever in the countryside, and how our farmers were adapting to new methods, albeit sometimes rather slowly! Regular entries of routine farm work, and battles with the weather and escaping animals, are mentioned throughout, but the entries shown here are just a small selection from these years.

Henry Roberts, farmer c. 1955

1948

Henry Roberts was a leading enthusiast of the Hampshire Cattle Breeders new Artificial Insemination of cows scheme. In September 1947 his cow 'Racer' gave birth to the first heifer calf born on the Isle of Wight from A.I.

15th July - Took Racer's heifer calf into Agricultural Show, the first from A.I. on the Island.

16th July - Flew from Cowes Airport to Southampton Airport to attend Hampshire Cattle Breeders meeting in Southampton, and flew back.

29th July - Picked up load of Kale, stopped to give horse a 'blow' (rest). When we started again and turned up hill, the hames slipped undone, and Warwick came right out of shafts and the wagon started to run back. Edward and I caught the shafts and ran the front wheels round, and stopped it. We got home alright later.

8th August - Very heavy gale, up to 70 m.p.h. Yacht 'Hope' in trouble off Atherfield. Blown round to Binnel. Nearly drowned the lot, 5 men and 4 women. Vic Salter and Jim Richards pulled two women out of the water before the Rocket Crew got there. Three drowned at Sandown same night.

23rd August - Jim White's wife 'Carrie' had a stroke while doing the washing up. Me and others carried her up stairs in a blanket. I don't think much of her, I expect it is a doner. (She died by the end of the week).

18th September - *Young Greville 'Five Rocks' married Sylvia Whittington, Bramstone. Smart affair; had Church bells!*

25th & 26th November - *Threshing out two ricks. Caught 82 rats over the two days. Corn not hurt too much so they could not have been there long.*

1949

1st January - *Edward got Dog Licence for his pup 'Wiskers'.*

4th January - *Arthur Sprake's mother died. She had been in bed 10 years.*

30th March - *Boy Scouts started tonight; Edward is going to help, had about 17 boys.* (Edward became Assistant Scout Master for a number of years).

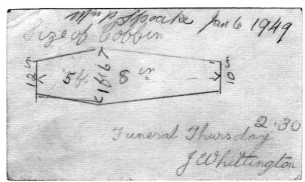

Card showing size of a coffin, issued to the gravedigger.

24th April - *Edward run up against Fred White and knocked him over down bottom of Chale Farm Lane. Hurt the motor bike a bit, but did not hurt White except from a bruise or two, and a cut on his hand!*

9th May - *Horses Dandy and Warwick got out last evening, went down road and someone put them in field. Edward and Roy White had a job to get them back this morning.*

7th July - *Vernon Barnes enquired if I would sell our milk round to Isle of Wight Dairies.* (No decision)

19th July - *Went to School Prizegiving, by Fred Hollis. Last as a Church School.* (The Isle of Wight County Council took over).

20th July - *Road men started covering in ditch along in front of Blacksmith shop. I asked them to put the bunny (drain) from Butt right down under the road, which will make it a lot better and the road can be brought up level. Helped them dig out the bunny.* (A bit of common sense in 1949 - in 2006 it would have required three engineers, two architects, and a six months delay to make a simple decision like that!)

21st July - *Went to Agricultural Show, last one to be held in Nine Acres Field. There were 4 four-horse teams, a good show.*

26th July - *Hilton Cheek gassed a wasp nest in garden with some petrol.*

5th August - *Old Will Bullock, about 75, down Chillerton, caught his hedge alight with a bonfire and got burned to death.*

6th August - *Edward killed two nice rabbits down middle field with one shot!*

11th August - *Carted corn. Put Dandy in shafts, and Warwick in traces for a change. Got on well.*

Henry Roberts - still using his horse c. 1950

Last week of August 1949 - *Thatching all corns ricks*

18th September - *Sid Cheek caught and killed Badger in Walpan Rickyard.*

28th September - *Edward killed 'Wiskers' (his young dog) as she is no good.*

16th October - *Heifers got out down Military Road, and Snowdrop was on the trot too over to Mayer's (neighbouring farmer) cows. Sid Cheek helped me get them back, then two bolted right back down the road. Got them back again, then some went in garage by shop, 2 in School and 2 in Clarendon, before we got all five back in yard!*

3rd November - *Dr Pridmore died. Rector asked if I would lay him out, but Raymond Barton and Jim Whittington had done it when I got there. Big man - 6ft 6ins.*

4th November - *Dug grave for Dr. Coffin 6ft 10½ ins long; grave 7ft 2ins; fitted very well, just room to get my fingers down each side of shoulders when it was in there.*

6th November - *Heifers got out again down Westside.*

7th November - *Heifers got out in morning. Got them back. Then got out in road again after dinner. Put up another wire along wall.*

8th November - *Heifers out again, found them over in School.*

9th November - *Heifers over in Clarendon twice today.*

10th November - *Heifers got over in Clarendon lawn; watched them all morning. Soon as I came in to dinner and went out again, clean gone. Two jumped over into Church Butt; then they got out down Military Road.*

11th November - *Heifers out again, down Military Road. I blocked up hole in hedge with thorns. - and again on 12th November!*

13th November - *Heifers went through Clarendon and away to Walpan. Put up an electric fence, and got them back after dinner. Next day - Heifers in alright this morning; I think the electric fence has beaten them. Then Harold Harding came in and said he had just drove the horses back, but they had now gone up Upper House way. They bolted right up over Hoy Down, wasted ½ hour before we got them back!*

28th November - *Sowed corn down Cricket Field with 'fiddle', and some broadcast.*

24th December - *Reg Choppings little boy died down Ryde Infirmary with appendicitis, aged 9 years. The news proper upset everybody.*

27th December - *Horses got into middle field, jumped railing this morning. Capt. Horsley phoned policeman to say they were in Pyle wheat field below his house!*

28th December - *Started grave for little Chopping, near telephone box.*

1952

6th February - *King George VI died. Record of his laying in state, and the funeral follow over the next few days.*

17th February - *United Service for King George in Church. Church was full, every seat. Bells were rung muffled. Horses got out this morning, found them down in field by telephone box at Newport Road corner. Edward went down and got them back this evening!*

21st February - *We all went over to Niton School to see Mr Waterman's film of the Isle of Wight in colour, it is very good. The old school was packed.*

26th February - *Hilton Sheath caught fire to his tractor trying to start it up. Heard him shouting for help, and I ran over as I thought his bull had got him. I chucked some dust onto it from the shed floor, but Jack*

Salter and Mrs Sheath had put some water on it before it did any harm; he had tried to smother it with a sack, but could not.

4th March - Heard that Cecil Lucas had died 7 months ago. Then - Wrong, still alive!

11th March - Budget Day. Things going up - Petrol 7 ½d a gallon. Edward got 16 gallons petrol today, saved about ten bob.

12th March - Dug out trenches for drainage pipes; took two loads of mud from outside stable to level it up. Alan Barton came down and we went through Club accounts. Made £7.14.0d, better than we thought. Both horses got out in garden again, and (next day) into Clarendon field dinner time.

14th March - I went to cut out some hay, got on thatch to tie it down and nearly fell off top as thatch slid away with me. Hung on edge of cuts but could not get back up so had to work over to edge and drop onto a cut lower down.

29th March - Rough day, six or eight inches of snow, and a lot of big drifts, snowed all day. No busses can get through. Went up round with Edward in motor with milk, had a job to get through up Blackgang.

30th March - Delivered milk with Dandy.

12th April - Big heifer keeps getting out, so put up another barbed wire fence.

1st June - Dandy had to be put down. He had been ill for a few days, and there was no hope. I gave him a drink of water once or twice from a bottle, and he 'wickered' for it when he saw me coming. Poor old horse, we are very sorry to loose him.

1st December - Tried to push straw bales off top of hay rick with prong, they came too sharp and struck my ladder nearly at the bottom and sent it sideways off the roof. I put my legs through the rungs and came down head first on the ground, and ladder too. Did not fall far, but far enough to kink me up pretty smart, also twisted my right knee a bit. Next day - 2nd December - Find I am pretty stiff this morning especially up round my neck. Good job I got off so light!

5th December - Richardson up garage by shop has got an old areoplane (his spelling!) They brought it on a lorry, drew in under our old elm tree out by blacksmiths shop and we put a sling and endless chain and block on a branch and lowered it to the ground, then we put on its wheels and pushed it up to the garage. The wings are coming later.

13th December - *Warwick pushed down old pig sty fence at end of stable and got in garden ½ past 11 tonight.*

15th December - *Frank Pratt* (the little boy that Martha Brown brought up in her cottage) *died in Bournemouth, aged 80 years.*

24th December - *Big steamer stuck on ledge just below Atherfield Point. Panama steamer 'Virginia'. Crew of 22 men and a woman. Yarmouth Lifeboat took off 1 man and the woman; Rocket Crew took off the other 21. They sent Dick Dabell out in breeches first to persuade them to come; they got them off very well. About six bottles of brandy and a lot of cigarettes sent ashore for crew. Customs bloke collard the lot as soon as it was landed, but it disappeared when his back was turned!* (She was towed off on 23rd January 1953)

1953

11th January - *Warwick got in garden last night and had a few savoys. And again the next day!*

18th January - *Bert Chiverton drove 5 or 6 cows up the road as he came to Church. They had got out of field and into Women's Institute field in the night.* (The W.I. owned a small plot of land near the Rectory on which they planned to build a Hall, but this was sold when they were given the Village Social Club Hall in 1953. In WW2 they grew potatoes there).

29th January - *Warwick and cows got over into Military Road, (and again on 30th January!)*

3rd February - *Man from Electric Light came about taking new line down to Chale Green from Military Road, and wanted to know who owned the land.*

At last the northern end of the village was to get electricity. Life in Chale was about to modernise!

Henry continued to farm at Denhams until his death at the age of 67 in 1961. His wife Octavia lived there until her death in 1971, aged 81. They had served Chale well.

CHAPTER 17

MORE 'MEN OF CHALE'

Whilst this book is aimed at recording the unique role of one family in the development of one village, others crossed their path, and without whom the Roberts of Chale would not have been able to achieve so much. I finish with a short record of the lives of just some of these people. Many others probably played as important a role, and their omission is in no way meant to lessen their importance - but you can't include everyone! In some cases I have included groups of people who together played their part in Chale's development.

JOHN & EMMELINE COOKE

Mr and Mrs Cooke were responsible for the education of the children of Chale from 1890, John Cooke being Headmaster, or 'Master' as he was called when he came to the local village Schools, (in the plural because there were strictly two schools, the infants, and the main school for older pupils). Mrs Cooke also taught in the schools, and on her husbands retirement in 1923 she became the Head Teacher for just over one year.

In his early days at the Schools, John Cooke worked with Martha Brown, and no doubt they made a formidable pair. Discipline under his control was paramount, and his temper was by reputation even worse when he had had his beard trimmed! The boys had to look out when he had been to the barbers.

Henry and Ridley Roberts, the two sons of Tom and Grace Roberts of The Clarendon Hotel, situated immediately opposite the school house where the Cookes lived, were both pupils of John Cooke. By the numerous letters written to Henry whilst he was in the Great War by Mrs Cooke, and occasionally by Mr Cooke, they were held in some regard. The tone of the letters from Mrs Cooke were both kindly, friendly, and amusing. In one she referred to another former pupil having written to the Cookes' using the term 'Dear E' as most amusing - "...we both had a good laugh when we saw that...". But excellent teachers they both were, and I am sure they had the best interests of their pupils at heart at all times.

They had four children of their own, all brought up in their parents schools; Cyril, Harold, Ada, and Norah, all apparently popular with their fellow pupils. In 1923, Cyril Cooke left home and started a bus and carriers business from Newchurch and became popular with his numerous customers. In 1929 he went to Canada on marriage, and returned to Chale in the late 1930's, when he visited many of his old friends. This included Henry and Octavia Roberts. Edward, their son, told me several times that he was shocked when, on departing, Cyril Cooke kissed his mother on the cheek. This was unheard of in those days, and Edward remarked his consternation was because "only Dad was allowed to kiss Mam"!! They never corresponded with Cyril Cooke again because of this indiscretion!

Whilst in Office at Chale, Mr Cooke had as teachers under his control, two of Octavia's sisters, Arabella Sprake (who left on marriage), and Julia Sprake (who continued as a full time teacher for many years until growing deafness meant that she was no longer employable (in those days), and she remained a spinster. This close professional association with the Sprake family led to a close friendship between these families.

Emmeline and John Cook - in retirement c. 1930

But Mr Cooke did far more for Chale. Principally he will be remembered for starting Scouting in Chale and encouraging its expansion across the Island from the early days of the Scouting movement. No doubt he met, and probably knew, Baden Powell, the founder of the movement. He was involved with the building of Chale's own Scout Hut, or Hall as it was called for many years. This, with the Village Club, situated close to each other, and within a couple of hundred yards of the School, provided the people of Chale with invaluable facilities to engage in social activities.

John Cooke was the Treasurer and Secretary of Chale Athletic Sports Committee before the 1914-18 War, and after was a 'handicapper' at the Cottage Garden Show and Sports which took over and ran the early Flower Shows (the forerunner of Chale Show) from 1920. Amongst other roles after retirement he was Secretary to The Chale Bull Society, and of the Chale Reading Room Committee.

He retired in 1923, and his wife took over the Headship for a year or so until she also retired in November 1924. At her retirement presentation in the School a gathering of local dignitaries listened with interest to the words of the highly respected Rector's wife, Mrs Charlotte Heald, who spoke of Mrs Cooke's widespread influence in the parish due to her unselfish and devoted service. Her tact, thoughfulness, and kindness had won the admiration and affection of many friends. The Rector endorsed these sentiments; a pupil presented Mrs Cooke with a fern stand and an autograph book signed by all the pupils; and Mrs Heald emotionally presented her with the main gifts of an illuminated address, and a Chesterfield Sofa.

Then Mrs Heald dropped down dead.

Well, almost. As the press report somewhat dramatically recorded, Mrs Heald, "...possibly as a result of her own emotion at the parting, was seized with an apoplectic attack, and was caught by those near as she was falling..." They carried her out into the fresh air in an attempt to revive her, but she died shortly afterwards having been taken home to The Rectory.

REV. CHARLES and MRS CHARLOTTE HEALD

That sad incident draws me to the second of the other 'Men of Chale', this respected Rector and his wife.

The Reverend C.W. Heald took over the living of Chale in 1888 following the untimely death of his brother-in-law, the Rev. William Rhodes, and married a 'local girl', Charlotte Jolliffe, daughter of Mr J.Jolliffe of Shorwell, and niece of Dr. W.J. Jolliffe, in 1894. Grace Roberts was companion to Mrs Rhodes and had lived at The Rectory with her and Charles Heald until her marriage in 1892 to Tom Roberts. Mrs Heald threw herself into all the duties of a Rector's wife. She was for many years a voluntary organist at the Church, both before and after her marriage, and there was no doubt that this had led to more than hymns being played on the organ. But it was her ability to say the right thing at the right moment that endeared her to all who she met, and her ability to make compassionate speeches led to her being a valued member of the Winchester Diocesan and Ruri-Decanal

Rev. Charles Heald - Rector of Chale
1888 - 1924

Conferences. She was the leader of the District Nursing Association, and no doubt encouraged Octavia Sprake to become a Wartime Red Cross Nurse. "By her death the parish of Chale lost an unselfish worker for good; and a high-minded noble woman".

The Rev. Heald, had great support from his wife, but became much loved by all in Chale throughout his nearly 40 years incumbency. He saw the village through the sorrow of the deaths of so many of his younger congregation in the War; and was partly responsible for the memorials erected in the Church to their memory, including the War Memorial in the churchyard. He wrote regularly to Henry Roberts whilst he was serving in the Army. He was involved in many village activities, and was Chairman of the Chale Sports General Committee before the War, and was the President of the Show and Athletics Committee when it was started again in 1920.

He retired soon after his wife's death and died in 1930, and is buried in Chale Churchyard.

HERBERT CHIVERTON

Herbert Chiverton was a pupil of Martha Brown, and he was the gardener at Chale Rectory throughout the time the Rev. Heald was Rector; he became the Parish Clerk; and he was the Sexton and Verger for some 42 years.

Herbert Chiverton

Herbert was born in 1873, the son of the Carrier, Thomas Chiverton of Blackgang, but it was to horticulture that he turned. On marriage he lived at Lowcliffe, before it eventually succumbed to the ravages of the sea. He became the gardener at The Rectory, where he had some four acres of gardens to attend to. So respected was he, that in 1897 Rectory Cottage was built specially for him opposite The Rectory, in Rectory Field. As with others, he too was a handicapper with Chale Athletic Sports before the First World War, and when the Flower Show was started, he became a regular and successful exhibitor and prize winner at Chale Shows until his death, and also at many other Island and mainland shows. He was a member of the Horticultural Society Committee and its Vice-Chairman for some years.

With Henry Roberts as Treasurer, Herbert Chiverton was Secretary of the Chale Village Club from 1919 for 25 years. He was also the head launcher of the Atherfield Lifeboat Station, and later a member of the Blackgang Life Saving Company. He was a member of Chale Cricket Team. But it was his work for Chale Church for which he will be remembered by many. He was a member of the Church Choir for 73 years, and one of the first team of ringers when the Church Bells were re-hung in 1897. He was appointed Captain, and rang the bells for many years afterwards. It was he who encouraged Henry Roberts to become a bellringer.

In his role as Sexton and Verger of Chale Church he was also the grave digger, a role which both Henry and Edward Roberts were to take on as Herbert got older. On his retirement in 1957, Edward Roberts became the Sexton. Herbert Chiverton had served under six Rectors, and in 1952 he had been admitted to the ancient office of Parish Clerk, the last person to hold the office at Chale.

The gardens at Chale Rectory whilst Herbert was there were a show piece, and it was perhaps fitting that God chose to take him home whilst he was cutting the hedge in his garden, shortly before his 90th birthday. Another worthy 'Man of Chale'.

ALFRED SPANNER

Alfred Spanner's life had similarities to that of Herbert Chiverton, and his involvement in the Church, the Schools, in Horticulture, in bellringing, in the Church choir also brought him in close contact with both Tom and Henry Roberts.

In early life he was a friend of Charles and Oscar Sprake, and was part of the Sprake's Mackerel crews from Ladder Chine. He was with Charley and a Charles Chick in 1873, when, returning from Freshwater where they had taken a catch of Mackerel, the sail got stuck and Alfred Spanner climbed up the mast, upset the boat, and my great-grandfather was drowned.

Like Herbert Chiverton, Alfred Spanner was a pupil of Martha Brown, and he too was a bellringer at Chale from the time the bells were re-hung in 1897 until shortly before his death in 1926. He also encouraged Henry Roberts to ring. He was a member of the Church Choir. He was a foundation Manager of the Schools where his advice and experience was gratefully received. He was one of the first members of Chale Parochial Church Council. He served for many years on the Parish Council, and was several times its Chairman. He was a keen sportsman and a judge at the Athletic Sports, and a Committee member of the Horticultural Show. It was his enthusiasm that helped make the Show the success it was (and still is). But it was for the School, and young people, that Alfred Spanner will probably be remembered.

Alfred Spanner left money in his Will to provide the school with a playground, and the old playground shelters which older residents will remember. He left money in Trust, the income to be used to support young people of Chale, and this still exists; sadly inflation has diminished its value but it can still help our younger generation. A wheeled bier stands in the Church as a memorial to Alfred Spanner.

But those who now live at Spanner's Close on Chale Green should always remember that it was Alfred's family who owned and farmed land in Chale for centuries, after whom their homes are named. Another fine old 'Man of Chale'

CHALE CRICKET TEAM

Standing: J. Washer, W. Woodford, C. Wheeler, B. Pinnock, W. Harper Cooke, D. C. Dabell, R. Burt, W. Chiverton, H. Lowe, E. Wheeler, Station Officer Weeks, F. Sturmey, Coast Guard Sutton, R. Reynolds. Seated: G. Wheeler (Captain), A. Wheeler, J. Hicks, H. Chiverton, E. Howe, V. Hardy.

When Henry Roberts bought 'Chicket Field' near the seaward end of The Terrace, at Lowcliffe, in 1936, it was the only parcel of land which he bought himself (the rest was inherited) so he always had a particular affection for that field, in total some five acres. Now it is mainly lost to cliff erosion. But this was the home of Chale Cricket Team, and surely they must all be regarded as true 'Men of Chale'. (And so indeed should all those who represented Chale at Football over the years).

The picture shows the team around 1900, and some of the names have already appeared in these pages.

WALTER WOODFORD, and the Atherfield Lifeboat Crews

One name in that team is W. Woodford. Walter Woodford was to live in one half of Denhams, the Roberts family home, and as such was a close friend and associate of the Roberts family. He too was another pupil of Martha Brown at Chale Schools.

It is Walter's involvement in the Atherfield Lifeboats for which he will forever be remembered. He was a member of the crew of the 'Catherine Swift' which, with the other 'Back of the Wight' lifeboats, so heroically saved the passengers and crew of the 'Eider' in 1892, and which proved so beneficial to young Tom and Grace Roberts who had just taken over the Management of The Clarendon

The launch of the second Atherfield Lifeboat - The Gem 1907

Hotel. In 1907, the second boat 'The Gem' was launched at Atherfield, and Walter Woodford took his place in her crew, eventually serving throughout the whole of the time that a lifeboat was stationed at Atherfield.

Walter Woodford had married Emily Mew, a daughter of Simon Mew the grandfather of Fred Mew, the famous author of 'Back of the Wight'; professional at Chale Golf Club; and himself another 'Man of Chale'. The Woodford's lost their only son, Courtney, killed in the Great War in France.

Walter Woodford - a member of the crew of the Atherfield Lifeboat throughout its existence

Industrial accidents are always a topic of interest these days, but in earlier years the cause was sometimes different. In 1916 Tom Ridett, a Chale Carrier, was bit by his horse in his side tearing the muscles, and he was told by his doctor not to do any work until it was better. In true Chale tradition, others stepped in to help, and Walter Woodford took over for a few weeks running his business. In a letter to Henry Roberts, Mrs Woodford wrote that "Walter has been Carrier for the last few weeks..." and "...I think Tom will be back to work soon, and Walter won't be sorry as he has a lot more work waiting for him to do". People put others first and themselves second in an emergency!

The Woodfords were regular worshippers at Chale Church, and during the Second World War Mrs Woodford was a valued member of the home knitting section of the Chale branch of the Red Cross and St John's Central Hospital Supply Service, knitting over 50 garments during the conflict.

But it is to all those who risked their lives in the Atherfield Lifeboat, including Walter Woodford, that I dedicate their names as 'Men of Chale'.

There is no end to a story such as this, it is endless, and every community all over our Island has its unsung heroes. There were many more in Chale, but few families can have a better claim to have influenced the path of history of our village, and who deserve the accolade - 'Men of Chale' - than the Roberts family of Chale.

Chale · Isle of Wight

1. This is the last and only Will of Me; <u>Simon Mew</u> labourer formerly residing at Southdown Chale, but now residing at Blythes cottages Chale.

2. I bequeath to <u>Walter Woodford</u> — the husband of my daughter Emily — with whom I am now living at Blythes cottages Chale, the whole of my furniture and effects, to be delivered to him immediately after my death, with the exception of the oak chest.

3. To my son Thomas Mew residing at Southdown Chale, I bequeath the oak chest, to be delivered to him immediately after my death.

4. In witness thereof I have, in the presence of the two subscribing witnesses, made my mark X, thus, acknowledging as my signature, the signature at the end of This my will, this 2 day of February 1899

    Simon Mew X his mark.

5. Signed by the said Testator as his last and only Will, in the presence of us, both present at the same time, who, by his request, in his presence & in the presence of each other have hereunto subscribed our names as witnesses.

John Cooke
Schoolmaster
Chale School.
Isle Wight

George Cheek.
Carrier
Upper Bramstone.
Chale Isle Wight

"A Chale Will"
- Simon Mew

dated
Feb 2nd 1899.

185

Hoy Monument, was known as the Obelisk

Pepper Pot, was known as Pepper Box

Children's displays in Chale

Opposite page - Blackgang Chine from Lowcliffe c. 1900

Wreck of the Nimrod

The Sprake mackerel fishermen at ladder

The crew of the Nimrod outside the Clarendon Hotel

Whale at Atherfield 1924

Blackgang Chine Bazaar/Museum c. 1870

Blackgang Chine

Blackgang Chine access to beach c. 1880

Making the rick